## WHAT OTHERS ARE SAYING ABOUT THIS BOOK:

*"For all educators, government officials and, especially, parents involved with the deafened, Mr. Bertling and his contributors, all highly regarded professionals, offer startling and substantial evidence, scientifically and logically and yet reasonably to prove that the Bilingual/Bicultural ASL track does not produce educated, literate children. Here is an indispensable, convincing and definitive appeal to sanity and common sense, a stern warning of the pitfalls of ASL directed education."*

*-Arnold B. Adelman, Director*
**SPEECH AND HEARING FOUNDATION OF MASS., INC**

SOUTHEASTERN COMMUNITY
COLLEGE LIBRARY
WHITEVILLE, NC 28472

NORTH CAROLINA
STATE BOARD OF COMMUNITY COLLEGES
LIBRARIES
SOUTHEASTERN COMMUNITY COLLEGE

# AN INTELLECTUAL LOOK AT ASL

"Tom Bertling keeps the pot boiling in this lively discussion of ASL and its place in bilingual education of deaf and hard of hearing students, cochlear implants, and other hot topics in our field. Whether one agrees with the various writers or not, the perspectives they present are very important for everyone in teaching, parenting, or otherwise working with our youth to consider."

-Gerilee Gustason, PhD, Professor
**SAN JOSE STATE UNIVERSITY**

"This book should be read and pondered upon by anyone who is perplexed about the merits and demerits of ASL (and ISL -- Irish Sign Language) in education of deaf children. Even the pro-ASL/ISL protagonists will do well to approach the book with an open mind. This recommendation arises from acknowledging the all important right of the deaf child to education that will achieve equality with the hearing child. Throughout the concise book are many, many quotable and revealing points that should clarify for some people the reality of the issues that are unnecessarily surrounded by controversy."

-Stan Foran, Editor
**CONTACT (IRELAND)**

# AN INTELLECTUAL LOOK AT ASL

*"Once again, Editor Tom Bertling has done a remarkable job. Everyone with any relationship to hearing loss should read "An Intellectual Look at ASL." The more intense that relationship, the more important it be read. Highly educational and written in an easy to read style, this book is vital for parents of a deaf child and for those involved in funding for programs for the Hearing Inpaired."*

-Warren T. Hanna, Exec. Director
**HARD OF HEARING ADVOCATES**

*"As a teacher and a professor for 25 educational years, it has been discernible to read the change of hundreds of students' writings from English to ASL. I highly recommend Editor Tom Bertling who is fluent in ASL and from a long lineage of hereditary deafness. He provides honest discourse on ASL and education of the deaf for parents, educators, administrators and professionals involved with the deaf."*

-Prof. Frances M. Parsons, Author
**GALLAUDET UNIVERSITY** *(Retired)*

# AN INTELLECTUAL LOOK AT ASL

**EDITOR'S NOTE:**
   Notes of appreciation go to Arnold Adelman, Thomas Balkany, Paulette Caswell, Warren Estabrooks, Kenneth Goodman, Annelle Hodges, Bettina Menzel, Frances Parsons, Edward Scouten, Eleanor Scouten and Patrick Seamans. Special thanks to Valerie Jo and Rikki Sage as always.


**PUBLISHER'S NOTE:**
   The opinions voiced by the contributors to this book are theirs alone and do not necessarily reflect those held by the publisher or the publishing company. We do support one's right to express an opinion and we stand behind all our writers in this regard. We strongly support our society's intolerance for censorship and wholly oppose any attempt to impose restrictions on our rights to free speech and freedom of the press.
   There is very little agreement among all the factions involved in the education of the deaf child. Parents must explore all possibilities and options, then make the best decision for **their** child.
   It is not our intent to identify or ridicule anyone personally in this book. Only individuals who have already publicly spoken out or have become part of the published public record may have been identified.


**KODIAK MEDIA GROUP:** Publishers of vital educational and scholastic material. Available domestically and worldwide through most major school and library book wholesalers and distributors, internet book websites, or you may contact the publisher directly. Large quantity educational discounts available.

AN INTELLECTUAL LOOK AT ASL

# AN INTELLECTUAL LOOK AT AMERICAN SIGN LANGUAGE

*Clear Thinking on American Sign Language, English, and Deaf Education by:*

THOMAS BALKANY, ANNELLE HODGES, & KENNETH GOODMAN

TOM BERTLING

OTTO MENZEL

EDWARD SCOUTEN

Edited by TOM BERTLING

KODIAK MEDIA GROUP

# AN INTELLECTUAL LOOK AT ASL

First edition published 2001

10  9  8  7  6  5  4  3  2  1

Copyright 2001 by Kodiak Media Group

All rights reserved. Published in the United States of America. No part of this book may be reproduced in any form without written permission from Kodiak Media Group. Permission is granted for brief quotations to be used in articles of review, with the stipulation that credit be granted to the publishing company, and the name and address be included with the quotations used.

Copyright ownership of some of the material contained in this book may have been retained by the authors (and/or other publishers) and is/are identified at the end of each section reprinted.

For further information contact:   KODIAK MEDIA GROUP
P.O. Box 1029-B4
Wilsonville, Oregon  97070

SAN: 297.9993

ISBN: 0-9637813-7-5

**U.S. Library of Congress Catalog Card Number: 99-76140**

PUBLISHER'S CATALOGING IN PUBLICATION DATA:
Edited by Tom Bertling.
An Intellectual Look at American Sign Language.
    Bibliography information.
        1. Deafness--United States. 2. Deaf--Education of deaf children.
        3. Deaf--Means of communication. 4. Sign Language and
        Linguistics. 5. Cultural issues. I Title.

*Kodiak Media Group is a privately-owned company and receives no private or public (including non-profit) special-interest funding or grants.*

# AN INTELLECTUAL LOOK AT ASL

# CONTENTS

**INTRODUCTION** 8

**CHAPTER ONE**
*CAN ENGLISH BE TAUGHT TO THE DEAF USING AMERICAN SIGN LANGUAGE? by Tom Bertling* 9

**CHAPTER TWO**
*ASL, ENGLISH AND EDUCATING THE DEAF: A CLOSER SCRUTINY, by Otto Menzel, PhD.* 51

**CHAPTER THREE**
*THE ENGLISH ASPECT OF CURRICULUM FOR THE DEAF, by Edward L. Scouten* 69

**CHAPTER FOUR**
*COCHLEAR IMPLANTS FOR YOUNG CHILDREN: ETHICAL ISSUES, by Thomas Balkany, MD., Annelle V. Hodges, Ph.D., & Kenneth W. Goodman, Ph.D.* 79

**CHAPTER FIVE**
*STATE RESIDENTIAL SCHOOLS FOR THE DEAF: A NEW ROLE? by Tom Bertling* 99

# AN INTELLECTUAL LOOK AT ASL

# INTRODUCTION

This book is an important collection of essays centered around American Sign Language. The contributors to this book are recognized for their critical thinking in their published writings. They are among the nation's top researchers, distinguished educators and notable commentators.

In addition to ASL, the contributors discuss deaf education, the importance of English reading and writing skills, deaf culture, ethical questions, Cochlear Implants, residential schools for the deaf, and the future for our deaf children.

Parents of deaf children, professionals and educators of the deaf, and members of the hearing society in general are awash in a rather one-sided view of deaf culture, and in particular, American Sign Language (or ASL). In short, things are not what they seem.

All of these writers venture into the heart of deaf language and cultural issues and reward us with the kind of critical thinking and skepticism largely absent from many of the proponents of ASL-based learning for the deaf.

Keep in mind that none of these individuals have called for the demise of deaf culture or the elimination of ASL usage outside the classroom. It would be (and has always been) a mistake to assume all proponents of English-based signing are "anti-ASL."

AN INTELLECTUAL LOOK AT ASL

# CHAPTER ONE

## CAN ENGLISH BE TAUGHT TO THE DEAF USING AMERICAN SIGN LANGUAGE?

## A Scientific and Skeptical Inquiry by Tom Bertling

*[Tom Bertling is the hard-of-hearing author of two highly acclaimed books titled: "A Child Sacrificed to the Deaf Culture," and "No Dignity for Joshua." In addition to being the editor of this book, he is also the editor of "American Sign Language: Shattering the Myth." Originally educated in a mainstream setting as a child, he was later sent to a residential school for the deaf at the urging of the leaders of the deaf community. He comes from a large 5-generation-strong "deaf of deaf" family and is quite fluent in ASL. While Bertling supports the usage of ASL among the deaf, he has serious questions about the usage of ASL in the classroom.]*

**AN UNPROVEN ASSUMPTION**

Can English be taught successfully to the deaf using American Sign Language (ASL)? That is the question being asked these days by many, especially when the issues relating to educating the deaf are debated. Is ASL a better method for teaching English to deaf children than using English itself through English-based signing methods, perhaps with oral

# AN INTELLECTUAL LOOK AT ASL

training? ASL advocates seem to think so. In fact, the ASL advocates' popular Bilingual-Bicultural method (or Bi-Bi approach), which is used in many deaf programs in our schools, is based on that very idea, which is: first teach the deaf in their "own natural language" (ASL) until they are fluent, then at that time, and only at that time, they are taught English through ASL. *[And, according to the Bi-Bi doctrine, speech training comes in only after the child is fluent in both ASL and English, but this is another story beyond the scope of this chapter.]*

Teaching English through ASL and not through English itself is an obviously extraordinary idea. It was the late Carl Sagan who was fond of saying: "spectacular claims must be backed with spectacular evidence." This statement aptly applies to the claims being made by ASL advocates.

Unfortunately, people seeking irrefutable evidence from the proponents of ASL and the Bi-Bi approach have always been disappointed. There simply is none. In fact, using ASL to teach English to the deaf and, in particular, with the Bi-Bi approach appears to be based upon *unproven assumptions*. What is more unsettling is that there does not seem to be much progress towards verifying these assumptions.

## CLARIFYING THE TWO TYPES OF ASL

Researchers have made the point that it is important to clarify the two types of ASL. This is necessary because most of what follows in this chapter and the rest of the book applies to what is known as "low ASL," or "foreign language ASL," the type of ASL that is favored by the ASL advocates.

Dr. William Stokoe, *[at the time a researcher at Gallaudet University]*, identified two types of ASL. The first is "high-ASL," loosely based on English, with unmodified ASL

# AN INTELLECTUAL LOOK AT ASL

signs in English-word-order with lipreading being the primary channel of communication, and a lot of fingerspelling. "High-ASL" is used with the various methods based on English-word-order. Researchers of today are encouraging the usage of the designation ASE (American Signed English) instead of "high-ASL" as a means of eliminating the confusion between the two types of "ASL."

On the other hand, "low-ASL" involves not signing in English grammatical order with very little fingerspelling. This is the "foreign language" version that is supported by ASL advocates. It is this version, "low-ASL," that I *[and our other contributors]* will be referring to throughout this book.

## A SKEPTICAL INQUIRY

Before proceeding further, a few words about skepticism. Many people associate skepticism with negativism. This is a mistake. Skeptics are simply seeking the truth, sorting the facts from the hype, to ensure that the claim is based on scientific evidence. This is a rather elementary step but all to often it is not taken.

Unfortunately, sometimes during the process of finding the truth, skeptics appear to be removing something without putting anything in its place. In matters that are a fundamental part of someone's life (such as language), response to this can be emotional and drastic. We have all experienced such letdowns in the past when we let ourselves be emotionally caught up in a fantastic illusion only to later discover the stone-cold truth. The result, then, is to vent anger on the bearer of "bad news."

Dr. Ray Hyman, an eminent psychologist at the University of Oregon, told of this true incident. Several decades ago he was teaching a course on the subject of

# AN INTELLECTUAL LOOK AT ASL

pseudopsychology *[not having anything to do with deafness]*. A student later came to him and said: "You know, Professor Hyman, as a result of taking your course I now realize how I have been fooling myself. And I see how others fool themselves as well. But, you know, I wish I had never taken your class. I hate your guts."

The moral here is that some people just do not want to know the truth. However, it is up to skeptics to ensure that those people with this kind of faulty thinking are not involved in leadership decision-making processes that affect *everyone*. This especially includes ASL advocates, who, after all, if they could have their way, would require *every* deaf child to use ASL and do away with any semblance of English-only education, not to mention oral education.

In trying to understand the shortcomings of human beings, Dr. Michael Shermer, a noted author, publisher and nationally recognized expert on skepticism, adopts the wisdom of the Dutch philosopher Baruch Spinoza: "I have made a ceaseless effort not to ridicule, not to bewail, not to scorn human actions, but to understand them." It is Shermer's outstanding book, *Why People Believe Weird Things*, a guideline on skepticism, that has provided the basis for constructing this thesis.

And finally, there are the inevitable naysayers who will say that "ASL linguistics" is not a "science" and therefore, should be excused from close scrutiny by us skeptics. To them, let me just quote Webster: **Linguistics:** 1. the *science* of language 2. the study of a particular language (emphases in italics are mine).

# AN INTELLECTUAL LOOK AT ASL

**WHAT IS SCIENTIFIC EVIDENCE?**

The scientific community over the years (and this certainly includes the linguistics community) has developed what is commonly known as the *scientific method* to prove or disprove hypotheses, theories and claims.

Without going into the technical aspects of what consists of "good science" while researching, what is universally agreed upon, is that the scientific method demands that *all claims depend on duplication for verification*. In other words, if an idea is indeed true, then anybody (not associated with the original research group making the claim) should be able to duplicate the research elsewhere and get the same findings. If the results cannot be duplicated, then the concept has to be considered false.

To take this a step further. One study does not make a discipline. Again, Hyman: "Proof in science happens through replication, not through single experiments." There is no better example of this than an incident which occurred in 1989 when two scientists, Stanley Pons and Martin Fleischmann from a university in Utah, in haste announced the discovery of "cold fusion." If this claim was indeed true, it would have lessened our dependency on fossil fuels, in short, be a major discovery. However, nobody throughout the world was able to duplicate this extraordinary feat. In the end, despite what Pons and Fleischmann claimed, their highly publicized discovery was proven false. To nobody's surprise, the biggest fallout for Pons and Fleischmann was almost irreparable damage to their reputations.

Also important: Claims lacking in evidence and plausibility but presented in a way that they appear scientific is *pseudoscience*. It is quite simple -- if it doesn't pass muster with the *scientific method* then the theory or hypothesis has

# AN INTELLECTUAL LOOK AT ASL

not been proven. No amount of scientific terms, references and language can make a false claim true.

Granted, research studies in social sciences (the study of human beings) such as linguistics, are on occasion a bit more difficult to replicate exactly due to the personality and behavioral differences among the participants. In this case, however, one can demonstrate statistically based on *outcomes* what programs or methods work, especially when comparing one against the others. But whenever applicable, the *scientific method* should be applied fast and often.

## SAGAN'S GIFT TO US: A BALONEY DETECTION KIT

The legacy of the late Dr. Carl Sagan, the distinguished author, astronomer and scientist, is his 1996 book on skepticism titled: *The Demon-Haunted World*. In this universally acknowledged masterpiece, Sagan provided us with 'tools for critical thinking' for our world of pseudoscience and deception. I have included a few of these tools that have relevance to language issues: (italics for emphasis are mine)

> Whenever possible, there must be *independent confirmation of the "facts."*
>
> Encourage substantive debate on the evidence by knowledgeable proponents of *all points of views.*
>
> Arguments from authorities carry little weight -- "authorities" have made mistakes in the past and they will do so again in the future. Authorities must prove their contentions like everyone else.
>
> If there is a chain of argument, every link in the chain must work -- not just most of them.

# AN INTELLECTUAL LOOK AT ASL

Carefully designed and controlled experiments are essential. Variables must be separated and experiments must often be "double blind."

In addition, Sagan teaches us what *not to do:*

Attack the arguer and not the argument. *[e.g., Verbal and physical abuse of supporters of English signs by ASL advocates.]*

Argument from adverse consequences. *[e.g., If the Cochlear Implant isn't banned, ASL and Deaf Culture will disappear.]*

Caricaturing a position to make it easier to attack. *[e.g., English supporters care more about hearing society than Deaf Culture.]*

Using "It happened after, so it was caused by." *[e.g., As a result of the 1880 Milan Conference, hearing people are to blame for the poor reading skills of today's deaf graduates of residential schools.]*

Appealing to ignorance -- the claim that whatever has not been proven false must be true and vice versa.

Suppressed evidence or "half truths, observational selection" or "counting the hits and not the misses."

While this list is by no means complete, it does provide a simple path to follow when examining evidence. As a champion of the scientific method and critical thinking, Sagan leaves us with these words to heed:

". . . every time we exercise self-criticism, every time we test our ideas against the outside world, we are doing science. When we are self-indulgent and uncritical, when we confuse hopes and facts, we slide into pseudoscience . . ."

Sagan also warns that if scientists are reluctant to debate or discuss matters with the proponents of pseudoscience, "pseudoscience can win the debate by default."

# AN INTELLECTUAL LOOK AT ASL

**WHERE IS THE EVIDENCE?**

Getting back to our original question: Can ASL be used successfully to teach English to the deaf better than methods based on English? A simple question, yet we have no answer based on scientific evidence. The ASL advocates, however, are thoroughly convinced that it does work, in fact better than through English itself. They have convinced a large number of well-meaning educators that this is the case as evidenced by the number of programs that have implemented the Bi-Bi approach.

However, a number of prominent educators have publicly expressed concerns for years about the complete lack of scientific evidence for this and the wisdom of plowing ahead with unproven methods.

In a recently published book titled: *American Sign Language: Shattering the Myth,* documents show that the late Dr. Larry Stewart, then a deaf professor at Gallaudet University, raised concerns as early as 1991 in several Gallaudet campus faculty memos regarding an "ASL-only in the classroom" movement *[at two national model schools for the deaf on the Gallaudet campus].* In one memo he said:

> ". . . the decision . . . was, for me as a member of the Gallaudet professional community, a source of great embarrassment, for it is nothing short of mind-boggling to note that the decision . . . to use ASL-only in the classroom, is built upon a foundation that is starkly without benefit of respectable substantive educational learning theory or solid prior research findings . . ."

In no uncertain terms, Dr. Stewart made it quite clear that research evidence verifying the claims made by the ASL advocates did not exist and that these advocates even resorted to mistruths in publications and the deliberate altering of

# AN INTELLECTUAL LOOK AT ASL

historical truth (which Stewart documented) intended to mislead parents of deaf children by creating an appearance of legitimacy. These two examples were in Stewart's memos:

". . . Frankly, we are worried that incorrect information is being distributed. For example, we are including a page from the 9/27 KDES *[Kendall Demonstration Elementary School located on Gallaudet's campus]* Weekly Parent Bulletin. The section begins, 'Teaching a deaf child the language of signs will help him learn English later, reports a research team from the University of Pittsburgh.' Later the researchers are identified as Stokoe, Casterline, and Croneberg. Now we know that Stokoe, et. al. were never at Pitt and they never did the type of research described! . . ."

". . . in a 9/3/91 letter to KDES parents and guardians a statement is made '. . . a growing number of research studies have described the power and strength of this language (ASL) for instruction . . .' Our problem, quite simply, is that we do not know of any research, with one exception, on the use of ASL for instruction. . . ."

Dr. Stewart in later memos to the Gallaudet and KDES faculty repeatedly asked of the ASL advocates the kind of questions one would face being scrutinized by the *scientific method*.

Another Gallaudet professor and author, Frances Parsons, also deaf, foresaw the dubious events surrounding ASL years before anyone else spoke out publicly about them. Renowned as Gallaudet's "ambassador to the world" and former avid supporter of ASL, Prof. Parsons later began speaking out against ASL usage in the classroom. As a result of her early convictions, she was frequently verbally abused and even once physically assaulted *by another Gallaudet professor!* Documentation published in *American Sign Language: Shattering the Myth* and other material on file in

# AN INTELLECTUAL LOOK AT ASL

the Gallaudet University Archives evidence the harsh treatment she has received from ASL advocates.

Prof. Parsons has succeeded, however, in helping ensure that the ASL advocates did not overwhelm the education of the deaf in the United States as many deaf programs still use English-word-order based signs. Overseas, where she is popular and highly regarded (and a frequent visitor), she has managed to hold the American ASL advocates at bay. Indeed, documentation indicates a significant increase in the participation of utilizing signing based on English-word-order.

Needless to say, neither Stewart nor Parsons, both renowned and respected educators of the deaf, ever saw the research evidence requested of the ASL advocates.

Today, a number of professionals specializing in these issues are pressing harder for answers from the ASL advocates. Published material with false or misleading information in support of ASL no longer goes uncontested *[discussed further in this essay]*. Even misinformation at websites has resulted in apologies from college administrators. Others are conducting their own research into the claims of the ASL advocates. Like many of my colleagues, we have requested in writing that various administrators at prominent deaf programs in schools and colleges across the United States furnish us with evidence showing the justification of their Bi-Bi or ASL in the classroom programs. *[I have yet to receive a response.]*

Today, more and more professionals are reminding us not to be fooled by the ASL advocates. Dr. Diane O'Connor, who while chairing the Gallaudet University English Department, stated in a Gallaudet publication *[The Buff and Blue]* in March of 1998:

# AN INTELLECTUAL LOOK AT ASL

> ". . . we have to keep in mind that there has never been evidence that one can learn English through ASL"

Also, Paulette Caswell, J.D., a PhD candidate majoring in International and Intercultural Studies at the University of Southern California, who has a keen eye on these matters and is actively seeking evidence supporting the claims of ASL advocates, insists that there is no evidence that "ASL can teach English."

Even some ASL advocates are quietly admitting that research supporting the claim doesn't exist. Stephen Nover, a noted deaf researcher, stated on several occasions that this was the case. I asked him to confirm these statements and this was his reply:

> "To date, there has not been sufficient research of the application of ASL within the classroom environment or how its use can support the acquisition of English."

Nover should be commended for going on record with this particular statement of fact. Nover did mention that he was director of a 5-year research project that was just underway and that one of the goals was to establish and provide this research. However, others claim that this particular research project headed by Nover is not going to provide the necessary answers and reasoning behind its undertaking is suspect and they also insist that there *has* been research and outcomes testing. But it does indicate that some ASL advocates acknowledge that research in this area needs to be done.

The fact of the matter at hand today is this: we have yet to see a single research study that shows beyond a doubt that ASL can be used to teach English to the deaf, resulting in English fluency comparable to the deaf child's hearing peers. This especially includes the results of literally thousands of deaf

# AN INTELLECTUAL LOOK AT ASL

children participating in Bi-Bi programs throughout the United States during the past decade.

### *Exactly what evidence are we looking for?*

Caswell explains it this way: English is a *phonetic, phonemic and linear* language, and it can cross over and be used to teach any other language such as German, French and Spanish. ASL, however, is a *nonphonetic, nonphonemic, nonlinear, and nonverbal* language. Scientific and professional research results must prove, with unbiased data, that ASL can be used to effectively teach a language properly and completely. *[A more in-depth guideline is provided by Caswell at the end of this chapter.]*

## SCRUTINIZING ASL RESEARCH, ASL THEORIES AND ASL ADVOCACY ACTIVITIES

I am directing my concerns at only some of these ASL researchers, educators and advocates (they know who they are). They actually constitute a small minority but, for the most part, they have a collectively loud voice. However, I am quite sure that there are more than a few deaf researchers who conduct careful and meticulous research and take great pains to be bias-free. There are also a number of ASL advocates who take care not to misrepresent their ideals. Unfortunately, they appear overshadowed by the conduct of those with extremist tendencies.

### *Inexplicable errors*

One the most elementary rules of conducting research is making sure the facts and figures are correct. Yet, I am alarmed how even the most prominent of the ASL advocates have published material that is riddled with errors. I'm not

# AN INTELLECTUAL LOOK AT ASL

talking about ordinary publications here. I'm referring to the kind of scholarly material upon which educators and administrators base their programs and curricula for the deaf. One example is Dr. Harlan Lane's widely referenced to book *The Mask of Benevolence*.

Lane is a scholar and is highly revered by many ASL proponents. In fact, he is one of the few *hearing* persons that has ever been made an "honorary member of "Deaf culture." With those kinds of credentials many would have no reason to doubt the accuracy of the material he has written. In this case, it appears that to do so would be a mistake.

A number of professionals have commented on the many errors in *The Mask of Benevolence*. These prompted Dr. Donald Moores, Professor of Education at Gallaudet, and according to Stewart and Parsons, a highly regarded "world-class" researcher, to say:

> "One of the most perplexing aspects of (Lane's) book is that it contains so many inexplicable inaccuracies and misstatements that are so obvious to anyone knowledgeable about education of the deaf. After coming across a number of these, I found myself unable to accept any of Lane's statements of "fact" at face value. . . . It is not my intention to belabor minor mistakes, but the fact of the matter is Lane presents inaccurate information too frequently for comfort."

Moores, who is editor of the *American Annals of the Deaf,* stated these comments in a book review he published in the *Annals. [These comments were also reprinted in 1998 in "American Sign Language: Shattering the Myth"].*

In addition, Patrick Seamans, a deaf PhD student at the University of Southern California, noticed that perhaps Lane made another glaring error while researching the original written works of the Abbe Charles-Michel de l' Eppe. Seamans

# AN INTELLECTUAL LOOK AT ASL

disclosed that in a chapter about the life of De l' Eppe in Lane's earlier book, *When the Mind Hears,* Lane stated:

> "Let there be no misunderstanding, however: as charmed as Eppe was to hear his pupils speak, he would never allow French -- spoken, fingerspelled or written -- to become the vehicle for their basic instruction."

Seamans says that this statement by Lane is quite the opposite of what De l' Eppe wrote. Seamans, whose first language is French, believes De l' Eppe practiced what we would call "total communication" in his methods of teaching the deaf. De l' Eppe included speech, speechreading, and fingerspelling as well as signs while teaching. Seamans noted Lane made no mention of De l' Eppe's "oral" method in his book. This is an unacceptable attempt to rewrite history for socio-political gain.

Needless to say, numerous inaccurate figures and statements in published research findings, especially ones that readers can verify elsewhere, can lead to a distrust of the other figures and statements within the findings, particularly the ones we *cannot* verify easily. There is an element of trust with the readers that cannot be violated. It further weakened Lane's case when Moores pointed out that many of the errors seem to be *slanted* toward strengthening Lane's arguments.

### *Questioning the authorities*

This is a step that we must never hesitate to do. This point was emphasized by Sagan earlier: "Authorities must prove their contentions like everyone else." We should never make an assumption based entirely on the statement of an "authority." In addition, Shermer gives this forewarning:

> "Authorities, by the virtue of their expertise in a field, may have a better chance of being right in that field, but that correctness is certainly not guaranteed . . ."

# AN INTELLECTUAL LOOK AT ASL

One has to examine the evidence to make the determination if the "authority" is indeed correct. Those who support an authority out of "blind faith" do so at their own peril. Our modern society has suffered dire consequences time and time again over the past few centuries as a result of "blind faith" in "authorities."

*The burden of proof*
Shermer also makes it quite clear about 'who has to prove what to whom?' He says:

> "The person making the extraordinary claim has the burden of proving to the experts and the community at large that his or her belief has more validity than the one almost everyone else accepts."

There should be no doubt in anyone's mind about 'who has to prove what to whom?' The conventional wisdom here is that one learns English through English itself. This has been stated repeatedly by educators and languages experts everywhere, including by both Menzel and Scouten elsewhere in this book.
If the ASL advocates insist that English is better learned through ASL than English itself, then the burden is on them to prove it.

*Claims based on anecdotes and 'rumors do not equal reality.'*
Reputable researchers do not base their research on anecdotes alone. There has to be corroborative evidence to confirm the claims made in the anecdote. Humans are flawed storytellers. We forget details and sometimes change the story

# AN INTELLECTUAL LOOK AT ASL

for the circumstances at the time the story is retold, two things that could actually reverse the expected outcome of a concept.

An additional concern to be weighed is a tendency within our society (hearing and deaf) to sometimes "accept rumor as reality." Shermer mentions several notable examples: Paul McCartney's death, George Washington's wooden teeth and that the moon landing being "faked." Many people believed those rumors even though they were never actually confirmed. In a society like the deaf community where both gossip and rumors are considered "mainstays," extra precaution is needed before taking anyone at his "word."

To take this a step further, there have been a number of published materials by deaf individuals who acquired some English skills through exposure to a mainstream or oral program only to later "denounce" the mainstream world and pledge allegiance to the Deaf Culture and the "ASL-only" ideology. Some have pointed out that one such example of this is Mark Doulsbraugh's book *Deaf Again*. While obviously Mr. Doulsbraugh is free to state any opinion he desires, this book (among others) has been used by some to "prove" that options other than using ASL for educating all deaf children are "wrong." Such books are anecdotes, not scientifically researched papers. While useful in bringing public or individual attention to specific matters, they are certainly not the basis for establishing or changing of an educational approach for the deaf.

The irony here is that most of the writers of these books and articles were fortunate to have learned English during their so-called "incarnation" in the mainstream program which allowed them to become fluent in English, something that most of their strictly ASL-educated deaf peers have no hope of achieving. Seamans describes this behavior as *corpus*

# AN INTELLECTUAL LOOK AT ASL

*planning* (an attempt by a group of people to change the language used to educate students, thus changing their perspectives on life and culture orientation), and says:

> ". . . hearing parents are being misled by ASL supporters by exposure to many "profiles" of "success stories" in prominent deaf-related periodicals. In many cases they received English-based education earlier in life and were already literate. . . these newly-created ASL users will later discriminate against and insult their own parents and teachers for teaching them to communicate independently in English, instead of having taught them in ASL, which results in functional illiteracy and a need to depend on interpreters for the rest of their lives."

Seamans, with many outstanding credentials, holds a Masters degree in teaching English as a second language, is one of those rare deaf individuals skilled in ASL yet skeptical enough to recognize the limited value of it in deaf education.

## *Closed minds*

A prerequisite for an open mind is absolutely necessary for researchers and scientists. One has to expect that during the course of investigation evidence may surface which may disprove the stated hypothesis. Being deliberately blind to contradictory disclosure is self-defeating, because during later scrutiny using the scientific method, the omissions become glaringly obvious.

We have to be concerned when prominent ASL advocates close themselves off from contradictory or at least interesting evidence surfacing at various public forums. If they refuse even to consider testimony or evidence brought forth in an open format, what goes on behind closed doors in ASL research laboratories?

Consider this: ASL advocates have always opposed the Cochlear Implant in young deaf children. This is not surprising

# AN INTELLECTUAL LOOK AT ASL

or anything new. They have opposed it for a variety of reasons, with several of the major ones being: (1) it doesn't really work, (2) it takes a deaf child away from his or her rightful "culture" and (3) there hasn't been enough "research" (which I'm assuming they meant that at the time they first brought this point up, no one was really sure if a deaf child could actually acquire a language (English) solely through the use of a CI).

They are flatly wrong about #1 as evidenced by hundreds of published CI research studies. #2 is more of a matter of opinion. Since the courts have ruled that ASL advocates cannot force their opinions on hearing parents of deaf children, it has rendered that argument wrong as well. Only on #3 did the ASL advocates have a possibly arguable position.

However, at this later date, there has been enough time to fairly judge the language acquisition benefit of the CI, and recent findings indicate that the prelingually-deaf CI recipient *can* acquire English with the device. For example: a recently released documentary *["Dreams Spoken Here"]* depicted a number of CI recipients who grew up with the implant. This included showing how 14-year-old Caitlin Parton, *[of 60 Minutes fame, who was the subject in an early segment on one of the first CI implants in a young deaf child. This was the segment that also ignited the "CI is genocide" movement by the ASL advocates]* and a few other early implanted CI recipients not only acquired English, but could speak it quite well. Even more remarkable, they picked up "hearing mannerisms" things that couldn't have possibly been "faked." Other follow-up reports indicate that Caitlin plays the piano and flute and sings in a chorus. Not bad for a child totally deafened at the age of 22 months from meningitis who was implanted with a device that the ASL advocates originally

# AN INTELLECTUAL LOOK AT ASL

claimed "doesn't work." The CI gives independent access to phonetics -- the basic requirement for English.

So what are the ASL advocates' position on the CI now? They are mostly just clinging to the "rightful culture" argument. They have simply closed themselves off to all irrefutable evidence which addresses their earlier fears of what they thought to be CI dangers.

For example: According to an article in the *Washington Post,* ASL advocate Harlan Lane stated at a public forum in 1997 that there was not one known case of a child acquiring language with an implant. After hearing this, a startled parent of a CI recipient offered to bring her 7-year-old son forward to demonstrate his fluency. Lane responded by waving her away and said: "With all due respect, madam, I don't need to meet your son."

What strikes me about this incident is that if this is how ASL advocates behave in public forums where they *know* people are watching (and documenting), I'm really concerned about what goes on behind the scenes when ASL biased books like *The Mask of Benevolence* and *Journey into the Deaf-World* (Lane is either the author or co-author of both) are being researched and unabashedly written.

It is important to note that in *Mask of Benevolence [on page 237]* Lane stated that 'because deaf children are a cultural minority' -- this is something that is not universally agreed upon by professionals working with the deaf, nor accepted by most deaf people -- 'we should refuse the cochlear implants for young deaf children, *even if the devices were perfect.*' (emphasis in italics is mine.)

The implications of this on ASL research is huge. They have already made the decision that preservation of Deaf Culture is more important than a young deaf child's right to

# AN INTELLECTUAL LOOK AT ASL

hear, and they have closed their eyes to any new or existing research findings that may perceive as being detrimental to deaf culture.

***Moral and ethical conflict of interest***

There is an ethical question that has not been addressed. Since most ASL advocates insist that *deafness is a culture and deny deafness is a disability*, it is a clear conflict of interest that the bulk of the ASL advocates' research funding, salaries and travel expenses is actually provided by society for *disability* research and teaching. In these circumstances, deafness cannot be *both* a culture and a disability. Nor should one be allowed to switch from one position to the other depending on which position is more beneficial *[especially financially]* for the circumstances at the time.

These ASL advocates insist "deafness is a culture" to justify their argument that ASL is their "natural language." This also serves as a means to preserve Deaf Culture. But at the same time they insist they are also disabled in order to continue to get the vast and various public funding that supports and nurtures Deaf Culture and provides legal disability protection (e.g., the Americans with Disabilities Act -- the ADA). This is a classic case of hypocrisy and I have yet to see movement by any ASL advocate to resolve this conflict.

In the view of many, taking public money earmarked for disability concerns and using it to support cultural activites is unethical, a sham and illegal. The ASL advocates have a long history of switching sides to get the best benefits of the moment. This is acceptable because we the taxpayers let them get away with it.

# AN INTELLECTUAL LOOK AT ASL

*Rhetoric over evidence, emotive words, bold statements and the devaluation of academic prestige*

There is a saying that goes: "As civilized as a college professor." In the midst of chaos one could always find reason and wisdom among our professionals at our colleges and universities. Unfortunately, tabloid journalism, verbal and physical attacks exist among some of these professionals. The behavior of some of the higher ranking ASL advocates has resulted in diminishing the respect for this whole field.

Others have engaged in rhetoric and have used emotional words which cloud clear thinking. To cite one small example: Dr. Ben Bahan, who is deaf and chairs the Deaf Studies Department at Gallaudet, repeatedly makes the comparison of the behavior of today's Cochlear Implant doctors to the horrors occurring during Hitler's Nazi regime *[during which deaf people were labeled as undesirables and many were actually sterilized, as well as murdered by the Nazis]*. At a recent conference focusing on "Deaf People in Hitler's Europe," Bahan used the occasion to once again attack the medical profession and CI doctors. He said:

". . . Could history repeat itself? *[referring to what Hitler did to deaf people in Nazi Germany]* The American medical system is threatening to reduce the number of Deaf people through cochlear implants and genetic engineering. . . . we cannot be like the Deaf people in Nazi Germany who colluded with their own *[destroyers]* . . ."

While ASL advocates may be using these tactics as a publicity tool, they have succeeded in harming the prestige and scholarly respect some have for professionals who have obtained advanced degrees. Bahan's need to equate Hitler's horrors with the hopes and dreams *[for new advances in CI and other medical developments raising the quality of life]* of

# AN INTELLECTUAL LOOK AT ASL

97% of the hearing impaired people in America has to be quite embarrassing to his more rational colleagues.

Prominent ASL advocates have also participated in a huge number of outrageous lies and contradictions in an obvious attempt to attract public attention and sway public opinion. Some of these numerous lies were thoroughly documented in an excellent research paper by Balkany et al. (1996), and to a lesser extent in one of my earlier books titled: *No Dignity for Joshua*. Just one example will suffice here: Dr. Yerker Andersson, who is also a professor at Gallaudet University, stated in an article that he wrote when he was president of the World Federation of the Deaf (WFD) in an apparent attempt to cast a bad light on the CI:

> ". . . *[an unnamed CI surgeon]* eager to use his skills on 17 deaf individuals. Three died due to complications and one became mentally ill. The rest were failures."

This was printed in the *WFD News* and none of it is true. The mind-boggling disregard for the consequences of comments like this leaves others wondering if the ASL advocates are on the brink of desperation or are so far removed from the reality of mainstream society that they have no comprehension of what is acceptable, advanced academic and scholastic decorum for professionals. In either case, or perhaps both, the need for skepticism and scrutiny are painfully obvious.

"Rhetoric over evidence" is a phenomenon not limited to ASL advocates. Jean Bricmont, a professor of physics at the University of Belgium, once stated at a conference: "A maximum amount of confusion in a minimum amount of words." There are scientists who, for one reason or another, believe in a theory without regard to whether it is true or false, and often avoiding discussing any evidence for their theories. This reality emphasizes the need to request and examine

# AN INTELLECTUAL LOOK AT ASL

evidence to see if there is any substance to the rhetoric being dispensed. Prominent deaf researchers have made note of this. Dr. Frank Bowe, a deaf man who was also the chairman of the Commission on the Education of the Deaf, stated in his well-known paper entitled *"Radicalism v. Reason: Direction in Educational Use of ASL,"* that 'We *[educators and researchers]* should base our work not on rhetoric but on research, not on radicalism but on reason.'

Empty rhetoric and bold statements are sometimes used to "legitimize" a claim. The simple fact that Bi-Bi approach was adopted by many educators and administrators without any research evidence showing that it does indeed work is a clear example of how a bold statement, in this case: *ASL can be used to teach English to the deaf*, was used to legitimize a questionable claim.

Stewart provided us with another example: In the early 1990s some of the Gallaudet faculty tried to adopt an ASL-only policy for some of the pre-college programs without conducting the necessary research to show that such a policy would actually benefit students. However, due to the efforts of skeptics like Stewart and Parsons, as well as outraged parents and elected officials, Gallaudet administrators scrapped the ASL-only policy.

Rhetoric and bold statements deceive in other ways as well. By having read some of the published articles and books written by ASL advocates, it was quite easy for readers to make an incorrect assumption that everyone using sign language is pro-ASL. This has caused some readers to become "turned off" and disavow any kind of sign communication *[including all English-based signs and Cued Speech/English]* to avoid any association with "those signing ASL militants!" In fact, the indiscriminate swinging of the ASL advocates'

# AN INTELLECTUAL LOOK AT ASL

"double-edged" sword has literally threatened potential sign users into remaining strictly oral. I am quite certain that this was not the ASL advocates' intention, but I have citations from eminent oral supporters that this is the case. It also is forcing a lot of deaf people into getting CIs, after which they completely drop out of Deaf Culture, with a great sense of relief.

The usage of emotive words by many ASL advocates is of rather common knowledge and also well-documented in Balkany et al. (1996). While I discuss these further elsewhere, one must take care not to get sidetracked upon hearing such words. Shermer reminds us that 'emotive words and anecdotes do not constitute proof but are merely tools of rhetoric.' An example of this: There is a tendency to blame the failure of deaf education on "hearing oppression." While there *used* to be some weight to this scores of years ago, one needs to take care not to become so clouded by these bold statements as to interpret them to mean "ASL is resolver of the problems in deaf education." ASL has to stand alone and prove itself, not emerge "successful" by default.

In concluding this segment, I would like to weigh in on the often heard claim: *ASL is the native or natural language of the deaf.* Caswell points out that this statement may indeed be true, but only about 10% of the time. Surely most linguists will tell you that a language is "native" to a person only if the person's *parents* use that language. Since more than 90% of the parents of deaf children are actually *hearing*, then for the majority of deaf children, *English* is their native, home language, not ASL. Only for children whose parents use ASL is this statement true. One cannot correctly apply this statement towards all deaf children. Even if there is a measure of truth to a claim, it may not apply to all circumstances and all conditions. Again, scrutiny will disclose all the facts.

# AN INTELLECTUAL LOOK AT ASL

It is worthy to note that "natural" languages in linguistics are *phonetic languages*. The ASL advocates are using the word "natural" in another sense, *not* in the standard linguistic sense. In general, gestures are "natural" to all human beings.

## *Confusion among the ASL and Bi-Bi Advocates*

There is a rather well-known phenomenon: People see things they expect to see in something they want to believe in, or as Sagan writes: "Wishing makes it so." Shermer on B. F. Skinner, the eminent behavioral psychologist: 'Skinner showed that the human mind *seeks* relationships between events and often finds them, even when they are not there.'

With this in mind, one could easily make the argument that certain deaf people are simply too emotionally attached to their claim and ideals to ever be truly impartial observers. For them, if evidence surfaces that proves their claims false, it may directly result in an adverse change to their lifestyle and well being.

When an extraordinary claim like the Bi-Bi approach is made and appears to be a politically-correct, "all things to all people" solution, popularity soars on the tag line alone. After all, how could one not be for *both* sign language and English? However, for some too emotionally attached to these ideals, one could forget to check to see if there is any shred of substance to all this.

If one were to ask around about some of the programs using the Bi-Bi approach, one would find mass confusion. Many ASL advocates and supporters simply do not understand the principles of the Bi-Bi approach. However, they will nearly "defend to the death" the system just based on the say-so of the few who developed it.

# AN INTELLECTUAL LOOK AT ASL

We must remember that there are going to be those who succeed with any method, no matter how "ill-conceived" it is. These individuals do not represent a "success" of a method. In our society there is a tendency to "remember the hits and ignore the misses." This is exactly why the scientific method exists. If a method is truly successful, that fact will surface under scrutiny.

## *Reversed Priorities*

There appears to be a lot of on-going "ASL-related research" but nobody seems to be asking the right questions. A great deal of time is spent researching to prove that ASL is a language in itself. One can hardly pick up a deaf-related periodical and not read about yet another study being conducted with public tax dollars to study the structure of ASL. Perhaps there is nothing wrong with this, per se, but shouldn't asking the basic question whether ASL can actually help the deaf learn English be of a much higher urgency? Because if it cannot, a great deal of this public funding should be directed elsewhere for research seeking alternative ways of educating the deaf properly and effectively to learn English, the language of our schools and our society.

## *Critical thinking going wrong*

We must ask: Are ASL advocates tainting research findings or interpreting data to fit their theories? All the data must be weighed into the outcome. Whether the data is understood or not or is just simply contradictory, it must still be presented. Data that does not support a hypothesis or claim cannot simply be "left out!" These omissions will reveal themselves during scrutiny by other researchers. This will result in, quite frankly, "egg on the faces" of the original researchers.

# AN INTELLECTUAL LOOK AT ASL

In addition, I'm wondering if there may be too much active participation in ASL research studies. The subjects being observed in a research study may change their performance to meet the observers' expectations. Even the knowledge that they are helping ASL research can taint the accuracy of the findings.

These are two good examples of how critical thinking can go wrong. Precautions such as blind and double blind controls must often be used to test a hypothesis. The participants in the study should *not* know the purpose of the study. Any findings obtained otherwise is faulty research. Such "informal" studies are often cited by some but cannot possibly be considered as a serious study if some or all of the participants previously knew of the hoped-for outcome!

*Professionals in fear of dwindling career opportunities*

This happens everywhere in our society so there may be a bit of human nature at play here. What if ASL diminishes in importance in deaf education? There will be a number of professionals who will not be able to transfer their expertise elsewhere. Caswell points out that many of them are under educated. In addition, even if they are academically qualified, some may simply not be able to function in other settings.

Human concern for careers and well-being is a fact of life and the possible influence of these personal feelings on research studies and advocacy activities cannot be overlooked.

We must keep in mind that our work in the deafness field is to better the future of deaf children. Sometimes this means sacrificing our jobs and careers.

# AN INTELLECTUAL LOOK AT ASL

*Suspect funding for ASL/Bi-Bi research and a mass misunderstanding*

The source of funding for most of the ASL and Deaf Studies research is our taxpayer dollars. Despite the huge clout and power large Deaf Culture organizations have *[such as the National Association of the Deaf]*, most of the funding for ASL research still comes right out of all our taxpayers' pockets, and this gives *everybody* a right to scrutinize how it is spent, and what the real outcomes are.

One has to ask: Exactly how did ASL, and in particular the Bi-Bi approach, rise to prominence in our educational programs, bypassing the peer review process? A number of people feel this is the result of several important circumstances, all without proper foundation. For instance, frustrated parents, often desperate, will accept anything offering a degree of hope, and become unwittingly supporters of dubious claims. The ASL advocates, now threatened by technical and medical developments undermining their "language and cultural gains," are making a last ditch attempt to reverse the tide, perhaps very much believing that their intentions are good, although their science is most certainly not.

It also appears that the Bi-Bi approach has become popular due to a mass misunderstanding on the part of the American taxpayers. For one thing, they have been convinced by the ASL advocates that Bi-Bi means *both* English and ASL. This is simply not true. As clearly explained by Menzel and others, Bi-Bi is mostly "pure" ASL until much later when English is incorporated only in specific "English classes." In essences, they treat English as a foreign language. Second, most taxpayers believe that ASL is American Signed *English*-Language, or a "signing version of English." Again, if this were true, who would *not* then be for ASL? If taxpayers (and many

# AN INTELLECTUAL LOOK AT ASL

educators and administrators) actually understood that ASL was in fact entirely different from English to the point where English usage is discouraged, disregarded and deliberately avoided, they might not have been so quick to hop on the ASL/Bi-Bi bandwagon and it would be most certainly a lot harder for anyone to obtain public funding for the extraordinary *and unproven* claims of the ASL supporters.

This leaves us now to ponder a legal and ethical question. Isn't it a clear conflict of interest for ASL advocates to use our taxpayer *disability* earmarked funds to HINDER medical and technical developments (in particular, the Cochlear Implant) for disabled American taxpayers? This is a question I have even asked of our U.S. Attorney General. *[As the book went to press, the U.S. Justice Dept. deferred the matter to the U.S. Dept. of Education.]*

Consider the facts: There are approximately 30 million Americans with a hearing loss, and I can safely say that the vast majority of them, including myself, consider deafness a medical condition, and we encourage all sorts of medical and technological developments to help reverse this condition. Examining the budgets at some of our publicly-funded universities (for example, at Gallaudet University, where federal taxpayers pay $78 million dollars a year to fund students who use ASL and who often "graduate" functionally-illiterate with a "bachelor's degree") will reveal that a good portion of taxpayer *disability* funding in ASL and Linguistics and Deaf Studies departments is spent on research, salaries and travel for faculty members who *insist that deafness is a culture and likewise spend a majority of their time fighting, hindering and suppressing medical and technological advances on deafness* and who use taxpayer money to publish and distribute this nonsense worldwide. We will, of course, hear the

# AN INTELLECTUAL LOOK AT ASL

"diversity" argument from ASL advocates, but the fact of the matter is that in most instances there is not equal funding to represent the views held by the 97% of deaf Americans who do not subscribe to the cultural view of deafness.

In most circumstances ASL advocates cannot have it both ways by claiming to be both a disability and a culture. However, it does appear that many of them do not seem bothered ethically with this contradiction of accepting taxpayer-provided disability funding and society-provided disability protection legislation (such as the ADA) while at the same time claiming that they are *not disabled* and are a "cultural minority" with their own "native" language ASL. With this being the case, the obvious recourse for us taxpayers now is to question the legalities of spending taxpayer disability money on deaf cultural studies.

## *ASL research papers: Anything really worth publishing?*

Just because another study on ASL has been completed doesn't mean it should be published. With seemingly endless funding available from taxpayers for ASL research, all sorts of "studies" have been done (except for the one asking if ASL can teach English). Some findings are simply useless and it serves no purpose to flood our academic journals with material that is just simply self-serving.

In fact, Sagan insists on this: Editors of scientific journals should ensure that the anonymous peer reviewers of these studies ask themselves: 'Is there anything in here that is sufficiently interesting and authentic to be published? Did the author do anything stupid? What are the deficiencies of this paper? Is the argument adequate?' Researchers everywhere routinely find it difficult to get their studies published, often for one or more of the above reasons. For instance, nine out of ten

# AN INTELLECTUAL LOOK AT ASL

articles submitted to *The New England Journal of Medicine* fail the peer review process.

ASL researchers should be held to the same standards. Worthless or useless studies should remain unpublished, no matter what the discipline is. There should be no special treatment just because the subject matter has to do with ASL or the researcher is deaf.

Readers should be aware that poorly researched or otherwise rejected papers often end up on lower-tiered journals. Papers published on the internet often have very little or no peer review at all. It is here where our critical thinking tools should be thoroughly applied.

## *Occam's Razor*

Occam's Razor is a scientific principle that simply means: With all things being equal, then the *simplest* explanation or approach must be the correct one.

Currently, with greater expense to taxpayers the Bi-Bi approach requires two sets of curricula, teachers and administrators. This does not include the expense of additional study and schooling time probably required for the deaf child's mastery of *two languages* (ASL and English) if the Bi-Bi theory is to be correctly carried out. Even if evidence existed showing that the Bi-Bi method was equally as effective as learning English the conventional way, it is still in violation of Occam's Razor.

## *The spread of professional level misinformation*

Professional journals and university websites have participated in spreading misinformation about ASL and English. For example: in the American Psychological Association's publication, *Monitor* (April 1998), the headline

# AN INTELLECTUAL LOOK AT ASL

read "Sign language may help deaf children learn English." Caswell noted the usage of the word "may." This was used, she says, because there is no proof. Looking further into the contents of the article, it becomes apparent that the writer doesn't really understand what ASL really is. Again, Caswell: "Are these people talking about real ASL, or are they assuming that ASL means signing in English? *[Low ASL or High ASL?]* From this article it appears that these people do not really know the difference between signing in the separate language of ASL and signing in the language of English." This is an important point Caswell makes because the difference between ASL and signed English is as different as day and night, and if the writers aren't able to see that difference neither will their readers.

Seamans gives us another example: At a Kent State University webpage, resource material indicates to hearing people that all deaf children MUST be taught in "signed languages" and in "Deaf Culture" and that they MUST learn the stories that teaches them the hearing world is "wrong" and "dangerous" and will cause their "imprisonment" (as well as even worse things, Seamans said.)

At another website, this time Brown University, the information indicated that "English" courses (for the deaf) are "conducted in American Sign Language," which is impossible. The website also contained other inaccuracies. Seamans sent a letter to Brown University asking, among other things, exactly how one is supposed to utilize a nonphonetic language to effectively teach the phonetic language of English. A Brown University administrator responded to Seamans admitting that they knew of no research "showing success in bilingual approaches to bridging ASL and English" and agreed to make some changes to clarify the website.

# AN INTELLECTUAL LOOK AT ASL

Conferences held by ASL advocates are also a source for misinformation. At a conference in 1992 held at Gallaudet University and funded in part by the U.S. Department of Education, Laurene Gallimore, who is deaf and is now a professor and the coordinator for the teacher preparation program at Western Oregon University, gave a talk titled: "How to use ASL as the language of instruction in the classroom." As Caswell reminds us: To do this is actually illegal in publically-funded schools within the United States where the language of instruction *must* be in English (except for foreign language classes). It also violates the ADA requirement of equal access to spoken information.

During an interview for a Gallaudet publication, Jamie Tucker, the popular deaf superintendent of the Maryland School for the Deaf, downplayed the value of speech. He was quoted as saying: "Speech is important -- but it is not language." One wonders, then, what is being spoken? Gibberish? To his defense, perhaps it was a one time faux pas, but the fact of the matter is, like Gallimore, Tucker is highly influential, and this kind of misinformation sometimes becomes widely accepted as fact.

In July of 1999, an article penned by Liisa Kauppinen, the current President of the World Federation of the Deaf (WFD), was published in the *WFD News*. To begin with, her "by-line" included a misleading title of "Dr." even through she has not earned a doctorate degree. *[In 1998, Gallaudet awarded her an "honorary doctorate."]* Knowledgeable professionals have pointed out that essay may very well be the most misleading, illogical, and as one researcher put it, "amazingly ridiculous" piece of "professional" writing they have ever come across. Space does not permit an in-depth

# AN INTELLECTUAL LOOK AT ASL

debunking but I will quote two passages that epitomize the professional misinformation she is spreading:

> "If sign language is forbidden or if interaction, teaching information and services are not available in sign language, a Deaf person does not develop language skills and cannot communicate."

This statement is so outlandishly incorrect that it is literally an insult to the millions of deaf people who learned to read and write in a mainstream setting over the years (including this writer) without the assistance of "Sign Language." This group would also include those from oral and Cued Speech programs.

> "When sign language is used and the environment is suitable for Deaf people, the disability decreases or disappears. Then a Deaf person need not be called disabled."

I need not make any comments on this one except to say that "amazingly ridiculous" is indeed the correct terminology to describe WFD President Liisa Kauppinen's writings.

## MORE QUESTIONS UNANSWERED AND POINTS TO CONSIDER IN CONCLUSION

### *Just how does one teach English using ASL?*

A number of professionals are wondering "Exactly how is this accomplished?" The late Dr. Otto J. Menzel, who was late-deafened himself, a former professor, audiologist and author of over 60 professional articles on deafness, mentioned how, particularly in a Bi-Bi program, they are not teaching English through English itself but by instruction increasingly being given in wordless ASL. Menzel reminds us:

> "It is impractical and inefficient to try to teach one language using another, when the language of instruction (ASL) is so

# AN INTELLECTUAL LOOK AT ASL

grossly different in grammar and in every other way from the language being taught (English). The goal is simply unattainable."

I might point out that Dr. Menzel was fluent in a number of languages and learned English as his *third* language after his family immigrated to the United States. Later, after he became deaf, it left him with a unique perspective on deafness and languages not available elsewhere. He often told this tongue-in-cheek but apt description how English should be taught to the deaf:

> "One does not learn to swim on dry land, nor does one learn English through American Sign Language. One learns English through English itself."

## *The ASL and Bi-Bi approach has too many other fundamental problems that need to be overcome.*

In addition to all the earlier concerns raised about the Bi-Bi approach, researchers are finding that the transfer of language skills from conversational ASL to English is problematic. In an article by researcher Eric Drascow, it is noted that a study by Mayer and Wells (1996) suggests the transfer of language skills from conversational ASL to English shouldn't be expected as ASL has no written form and ASL is not phonetic *[phonetics is needed to be able to read English, because "written English" is the representation of spoken English]*. Because of this, deaf students do not have existing literacy skills in ASL that can be transferred to written English. In addition, they point out the structures of the two languages are different.

Another major concern, mentioned by many including Bowe, is the severe shortage of ASL-fluent teachers. This would hamper the possibility of success for a Bi-Bi program.

# AN INTELLECTUAL LOOK AT ASL

Seamans indicates a number of other problems, which include a 30 to 40% misunderstanding rate (compared to Cued Speech) among peers using ASL. This is due to the fact that few can agree on the signs used, since many residential schools use different signs for the same concepts.

And finally, Caswell points out a reciprocity problem:

> "If ASL can be used to teach English in a bilingual program for the deaf" (as is asserted), then the same situation applies -- it should be possible, therefore, to effectively "Teach ASL by using English." No one in the world would ever assert that this is possible, because it is not. If there is no reciprocity, and if the statement cannot be reversed, then it is *not* a "bilingual" program."

### *Does the ASL-only doctrine include thought-crimes?*

In a thought-provoking article by Dr. Norman Levitt titled: "Why Professors Believe Weird Things," several points were raised about *Women's Studies* that can be compared with the behavior of some of the ASL advocates. Levitt discusses how some fields of study have doctrines that include "thought crimes." One such "thought crime" is to contest a current line of thinking.

This kind of "thought crime" is happening at Gallaudet University where a large percentage of the faculty actually does not agree with the ASL advocates running the Deaf Studies, ASL and Linguistics departments. They find themselves often "tiptoeing" around, being careful not to state anything contradictory to the ASL doctrine or they will find themselves battered with socio-political bombardment, and be accused of conducting "hearing oppression of the deaf." This fear of being accused of "harassing the deaf" could be viewed as a weapon used by the ASL advocates to force the "imperial aspirations" of the ASL-only doctrine.

# AN INTELLECTUAL LOOK AT ASL

There are other kinds of "crimes" and lies occuring as well. In 1992, Gallaudet English professor Truman Stelle went on public record detailing many of these in a stunning memo addressed to the university president and faculty. The memo exposed to the very core these crimes and lies being committed by administrators and educators of the deaf at Gallaudet. Stelle's memo was reprinted in *American Sign Language: Shattering the Myth.* Scholars today will find this memo a valuable starting point for setting forth changes in the education of the deaf.

*What should we say in response to dubious claims, deafness related or not?*

Elizabeth Loftus, a psychologist at the University of Portsmouth (England), stated that when someone tries to foist a claim upon you *it should be almost automatic to ask: What is the evidence?* Kenneth Morgareidge, a teacher from Colorado, suggests a common sense approach to planting seeds of doubt: Don't deny the experience but instead ask for lots of specific information and a step-by-step description. Ask for documentation and written material on the subject and ask for an explanation of technical jargon in simple terms. He says that often-times this process will make one less sure of his belief in a particular claim.

Of course, a direct confrontation with certain ASL advocates may be a fruitless endeavor. Besides, Menzel's humorous take on this was: "Never wrestle with a pig; you'll both get dirty and the pig likes it."

## VIABLE OPTIONS FOR PARENTS

Granted, educators of the deaf do not have many educational options available to offer parents. However, each

# AN INTELLECTUAL LOOK AT ASL

of the ones we do have prove to be arguably far superior alternatives to the Bi-Bi approach and "ASL-only."

**The oral/auditory-verbal approaches.** These oral methods do work at times, especially with hard-of-hearing children who are utilizing amplification. And now, with the Cochlear Implant, even profoundly deaf children (when implanted prelingually) can enjoy a high success ratio. Many totally-deaf children without the CI have succeeded with the oral approach. One need look no further than to Henry Kisor or Lew Golan, both distinguished newspapermen and authors and well-known examples of accomplished totally-deaf lip readers. Miss America Heather Whitestone is another. Unfortunately, not everybody can succeed with the oral approach, something the oral advocates have always hesitated to admit. In addition, some say that a very few "borderline" cases often result in deaf children that "look hearing" but are otherwise poorly educated perhaps due to too much emphasis on speech at the expense of other areas of study.

**Cued Speech/Cued English.** Originally known as Cued Speech, this method is the most promising, (aside from Cochlear Implant device) but perhaps the most misunderstood. ASL advocates despise it because of its association with "speech." Oral advocates hate it because of its reliance on "signs." The fact is that it is neither speech nor signs. It is simply the presentation of phonemes in English with a small number of hand-formed cues to identify phonemes that cannot be seen. This confusion is why many are attempting to replace the original name with Cued English.

It is most interesting that almost all preliminary studies and informal reports show impressive results. One can see the high English fluency skills quite easily in deaf students who were educated with the CS/CE method. Professionals who

# AN INTELLECTUAL LOOK AT ASL

have no reason to support CS/CE one way or the other have gone out of their way to bring this method to the attention of educators and parents. Even one rabid ASL advocate said off the record that "it appears to be working." CS/CE can also be learned by any hearing person in less than 24 hours -- a significant advantage over many other methods.

We are sorely in need of more options for parents of deaf children and I hope CS/CE can somehow overcome the public resistance to it and become a major and viable option since it results in 100% accessible English language acquisition.

**Signed-English.** At this time, the variety of signed-English or signs in English-word-order methods give a deaf child the best chance of becoming a well-educated deaf adult, able to cope in the hearing world yet still able to participate in a "world of his own." None of the other options allow for this. There are a number of variations of English-word-order with some of the notable being Signed Exact English (SEE), Total Communication (TC), and most recently, American Signed English (ASE) all which require "oral" and lipreading training. Another popular alternative is the Rochester method in which fingerspelling is used to supplement written English and speechreading.

Without a doubt, being able to sign allows full access to the Deaf Culture. If children choose, they can also learn and use ASL among themselves outside of the classroom. Bottom line: Fluency in English allows full access to the larger mainstream society, something that ASL cannot ever provide.

## *Words of wisdom for parents*

While many educators and leaders are divided over educational methods and ideology, parents should find some comfort that it is universally agreed upon that early

# AN INTELLECTUAL LOOK AT ASL

identification of a child's deafness is a key to the success of later education, whatever the method. In fact, it is critical. A recent study (Marcus et. al, NYU 1998) now shows that babies begin to develop grammar patterns as early as *7 months*. It is imperative that after the deafness is identified, a method of communication is begun *immediately!* Spending a year or even months squabbling over communication methods may result in needless permanent adverse consequences.

Our schools are clogged with deaf children whose parents choose to do absolutely nothing until they were of school age and then just dumped them on our educational system. This is a story beyond the scope of this essay, but the moral here is that deaf children having parents who care fare significantly better than those who don't, regardless of the method chosen.

### *A rational course of action.*

There is a distinct advantage to a deaf person having English skills in our society and this outweighs any level of fluency in ASL. Widespread knowledge and usage of ASL in our society is not forthcoming anytime soon.

If irrefutable evidence (and after it has been replicated by other independent studies) shows that usage of ASL results in deaf high school graduates having twelfth grade reading and writing skills, most of us will then welcome incorporating ASL into the classroom because we are by no means "anti-ASL."

ASL will always have a place among the culturally-deaf and most of us agree that nobody should try to take this away from them. But only scrutiny by the *scientific method* and professional examination should determine whether ASL should be used in the classroom, not by fallible human "authorities."

# AN INTELLECTUAL LOOK AT ASL

**REFERENCES:**
Arana-Ward, Marie, *The Washington Post*, (5-11-97), As Technology Advances, a Bitter Debate Divides the Deaf (Lane).
Balkany, Hodges, and Goodman, (1996) *Trilogical Society*, The Ethics of Cochlear Implantation in Young Children. *[Note: an updated version of this paper has been reprinted in this book. See Chapter 4.]*
Bertling, Tom, (1994) *A Child Sacrificed to the Deaf Culture*, Kodiak Media Group.
Bertling, Tom, Editor, (1998) *American Sign Language: Shattering the Myth*, Kodiak Media Group.
Bertling, Tom (1997) *No Dignity for Joshua*, Kodiak Media Group.
Caswell, Paulette (1999) Personal communication.
Drascow, Eric (1998) *Exceptional Children*, "American Sign Language as a Pathway to Linguistic Competence."
Holt, Robert Lee, *The LA Times*, (1-1-99) Babies found to Assemble Building Blocks -- of Speech (Marcus et al, NYU 1998).
Kauppinen, Liisa, *WFD News*, (July. 99) Are Deaf People Disabled?
Kendrick, Frazer, *Skeptical Inquiry*, (Dec. 98) Science and Reasons, Foibles and Fallacies (Bricmont, Loftus, Morgareidge).
Levitt, Norman, *Skeptic*, (Vol. 6, No. 3, 1998) Why Professors Believe Weird Things.
Menzel, Otto, (1998) Personal communication.
Moore-Levitan, *Deaf Life*, (Aug. 98) What "Never Again" means to us. (Bahan).
Moores, Donald, (1998) *American Sign Language: Shattering the Myth*, (Review of Harlan Lane's *Mask of Benevolence*), Kodiak Media Group.
Oberkotter Foundation, (1998) *Dreams Spoken Here*, Palo Alto, CA.
Parsons, Frances, (1998) *American Sign Language: Shattering the Myth*, (The Essays of Frances M. Parsons), Kodiak Media Group.
Sagan, Carl, *The Demon-Haunted World*, (1996) Ballantine Books, NY.
Seamans, Patrick, (1998) *American Sign Language: Shattering the Myth*, (Critical Thinking about ASL) Kodiak Media Group, and personal communication.
Stelle, Truman, (1998) *American Sign Language: Shattering the Myth*, (The Vison Thing), Kodiak Media Group.
Michael Shermer, *Skeptic*, (1998) (Hyman, Shermer).

# AN INTELLECTUAL LOOK AT ASL

Michael Shermer, *Why People Believe Weird Things*, (1997).
Stewart, Larry, (1998) *American Sign Language: Shattering the Myth*,
(The Essays of Larry G. Stewart), Kodiak Media Group.

## SUGGESTED CRITERIA FOR UNDERTAKING "ASL CAN BE USED TO TEACH ENGLISH" RESEARCH:
*(Contributed by Paulette Caswell)*

English is a *phonetic, phonemic* and *linear* language. ASL, however, is a *nonphonetic, nonphonemic, and nonverbal* language. Scientific and professional research results must prove that ASL can be used to effectively teach a *phonetic-phonemic-linear* language properly and completely.

Research must be from reliable and unbiased researchers who use traditional methods of qualitative or quantitative research.

All research studies should include the following critical pieces of information:

1) The hearing status of the parents of the deaf subjects studied.
2) Subjects' age of onset of deafness.
3) Subjects' audiological levels of deafness.
4) Whether the deafness is stable or progressive.
5) Type of education given at home (if any) by parents or caretakers prior to entering school.
6) Type of communication and language used at home.
7) Type of preschool and language used in preschool (and the same for all elementary, secondary and post secondary educational institutions attended).
8) Whether the educational institutions attended were mainstreamed, deaf-only day programs or deaf-only residential programs.
9) Information on higher education institutions attended, and accommodations used in the classroom, if any.
10) Showing of the actual audiology charts for each research subject.

It is important for everyone to recognize that research studies performed on hearing, hard of hearing or late deafened individuals DO NOT APPLY to prelingually profoundly deaf individuals. Identification of the items above is critical, to see if the professional unbiased research is actually applicable to prelingually profoundly deaf individuals -- the group that has the most difficulties learning a phonetic language (English).

AN INTELLECTUAL LOOK AT ASL

# CHAPTER TWO

## ASL, ENGLISH AND EDUCATING THE DEAF: A CLOSER SCRUTINY
### by Otto J. Menzel, Ph.D.

*[The late Dr. Menzel was a clinical audiologist, editor of deafness-related publications and a former professor who became deaf as an adult. Most recently he was the editor of "Life After Deafness" and has written numerous deafness-related essays including over 60 articles for professional journals. He was also the co-author of "Feud for Thought," a satire about the petty divisions among the many factions of deaf people. What makes Dr. Menzel's perspectives on language issues especially valuable to educators is his having been both hearing and deaf, both deaf and a deaf service provider as an audiologist, and his fluency in a number of languages with English being his third acquired language. Dr. Menzel was an amicus curiae extraordinare.]*

**ENGLISH, A GLOBAL LANGUAGE DENIGRATED BY ASL ADVOCATES AND DEAF CULTURALISTS**

In America, regional dialects are moving increasingly towards a homogeneous American English. At the same time, the rest of the world is rapidly adopting English as a second language, as the language of commerce and science, and English words and expressions are infiltrating other languages apace. The inevitable (and once unthinkable) is happening: The

# AN INTELLECTUAL LOOK AT ASL

world is moving towards a common global language and that language is English! The Tower of Babel is crumbling.

Meanwhile, in the Deaf culture, it has become fashionable to denigrate English, to downplay its importance. The Deaf community has come to believe its own propaganda about American Sign Language (ASL) meeting all of its communication needs, about ASL being as complete, versatile and sophisticated a language as English. The community believes that English is unnecessary for its deaf "citizens" since ASL is considered an equivalent for conveying the information and the complexities found in English. Nothing could be more absurd! (Note: The word "absurd" is particularly apt here owing to its derivation from the Latin "ab" [off or from] and "surdus" [deaf] -- literally, "from the deaf.")

American Sign Language (ASL) took on new importance after its "discovery" by Gallaudet researcher William Stokoe several decades ago. He ascertained that the informal gestural language, used mainly by deaf children among themselves and, in particular, at residential schools for the deaf, had its own grammar separate and distinct from English grammar. Sign Language had not come to be regarded as anything special prior to this. This simple observation, in some inexplicable way, gave rise to a kind of "deaf chauvinism" that has manifested itself, among other ways, in its pernicious effect on the education of deaf children. The move towards making ASL the official language of the classroom has been promoted through several notions: 1) that ASL is the "natural" language of deaf children, excluding all other forms of sign language, 2) that ASL is the preferred language of instruction in academic subjects, and finally, 3) that English must be taught only after the deaf child has been thoroughly inculcated with ASL, thus making English a secondary language. These notions have

# AN INTELLECTUAL LOOK AT ASL

nurtured the Bilingual-Bicultural (Bi-Bi) approach and, without scientific backing, are contrary to good sense. *[By definition, a "native" or "cultural" language is that language which has been initially introduced to a child at birth and which is used consistently as a communication mode through the first five years of his or her life. Therefore, to infer that ASL is the dominant language of **all** deaf children is incorrect.]*

## THE IMPORTANCE OF ENGLISH LITERACY

The most formidable challenge confronting any teacher of the deaf is to make the pupils literate in English. This has always been so. But the importance of it has grown substantially in recent years because of the impressive demands of the "information age" generally and also because of the technological advances that have affected the lives of deaf people specifically. Text telephones and relay services, closed captioned television, "on-line" computer services, facsimile machines -- all these have greatly enhanced life for deaf people and brought them closer to mainstream society, *provided they have reasonable competency in English and can read and write!* The information age is upon us with a vengeance, like it or not, and voluntary illiteracy simply won't wash.

How is the deaf child to become English literate? The typical graduate of a typical residential school for the deaf in America has reading skills no better than a third or fourth grade level, the bare threshold of literacy by general standards. Three out of four cannot read a newspaper.

Most deaf pupils in residential schools spend but a fraction of their time in English class! Unlike hearing children, they are not exposed to English outside of class, via family, radio, television, or playmates; neither are they likely to do any reading for pleasure since they have not learned to read. Under

# AN INTELLECTUAL LOOK AT ASL

such circumstances, how are they to acquire adequate English language skills?

**Language is best learned by immersion.** English, like any language, is best learned by immersion, by being surrounded by it continuously, by being forced to use it exclusively. This author learned English as a third language quickly and thoroughly by being placed in an ordinary public school setting where English was the sole language used for all purposes. There was no special "bilingual" instruction, no recourse to previously learned languages. One does not learn to swim on dry land, nor does one learn English through American Sign Language. One learns English through English itself. We all know that deaf children take to ASL naturally and easily if exposed to it at home (or elsewhere) on a daily basis in just the same way hearing children learn English without specifically being "taught." Exposure is the answer! But nothing does more for English acquisition than *reading, reading, reading*, and more reading.

**Knowledge of a verbal language such as English is necessary.** When a meager English skill is not nurtured, let alone expanded, it atrophies. Therefore, whatever level of English that exists in a deaf student must be encouraged, stimulated and built on until it reaches the highest level of proficiency possible.

Verbal language is necessary for more than getting along in society. It is necessary for abstract thought itself. Functionally illiterate deaf students would be unable to understand the subject matter, insofar as it relied on abstract ideas, as all truly authentic college courses do.

# AN INTELLECTUAL LOOK AT ASL

## SIGN LANGUAGE IN DEAF EDUCATION

Throughout most of the history of American deaf education, sign language has been used. Until comparatively recently, the several variants of it were largely based on English-word-order, such as "Signed Exact English," "English Sign Language," and "English Signs." These sundry sign languages were useful in teaching English because of grammatical similarity, supplemented at times by fingerspelling.

Despite statements from its enthusiasts as to the complexity, flexibility and expressiveness of ASL, the language is severely limited compared to English, quite incapable of expressing many nuances available to a person thoroughly conversant (pun unintended, yet apt) with English. Perhaps even more important is that ASL has no written form. There are no textbooks in ASL, no newspapers, no instruction manuals, no job application forms, et cetera. That alone tears it to rags and atoms as anybody's stand-alone language. In the contemporary world it is unrealistic to pretend that literacy and mastery of English is unnecessary. Nobody is self-sufficient today, not even nations.

Sign language is unquestionably an important tool for use with -- and by -- prelingually deaf children. Its use as a "first" language to serve as a stepping stone to English, as well as a means of early "bonding" with parents and siblings, has clear value. Its use, however, should never prevent, let alone preclude, the early introduction to English. Insofar as the acquisition of English as early as possible is a prime objective, any sign language used in those early stages should be one of the several systems based on English, and NOT ASL, possibly excepting the case of a child whose parents know only ASL.

# AN INTELLECTUAL LOOK AT ASL

## GALLAUDET UNIVERSITY'S ACADEMIC ACHIEVEMENTS QUESTIONED

The 150-year history of what is now euphemistically designated "Gallaudet University" is replete with deception to Congress and to the taxpayers of the United States, purporting to be an institution of higher learning for the deaf. In fact, even today Gallaudet admits students who are "half-fitted" and graduates them "half-educated," and even this is almost a glorification. (Further details of Gallaudet's sordid history can be found in Paulette R. Caswell, J.D.'s paper "Deprivation of a Single Sense": 139 years of Gallaudet University Fraud and Deception (USC 1996).

Admission to Gallaudet, even today, is open to students with no better than an 8th grade reading level, let alone reading and language skills commensurate with customary collegiate entrance requirements elsewhere. Predictably, more than a few Gallaudet graduates are functionally illiterate, and for those holding "degrees" from the Gallaudet School of Education and Human Services, many are assuredly not qualified to teach.

Furthermore, many Gallaudet graduates are not qualified for employment by leading corporate employers, a number of whom have notified Gallaudet University that they would no longer hire Gallaudet graduates because they cannot read and write even at the most basic levels of literacy.

**Unexpected consequences.** The celebrated "Deaf President Now" revolt at Gallaudet in 1988 has led to unexpected consequences. Quite aside from the more recently established facts about that incident, which show that the "revolt" was actually instigated by persons who were not students, there was also considerable distortion of the events by the media. Those events gave rise to some new, chauvinistic attitudes among both students and faculty. Somehow, the

# AN INTELLECTUAL LOOK AT ASL

events of 1988 gave rise to "deaf pride" and "Deaf Culture," both of which are political creations, not anthropological realities. They also gave rise to a fanatical movement, supported by both students and faculty and tolerated by a weak administration. This further segregated the deaf from the mainstream of American society.

Among the incomprehensible but strong advocacies of these radicals is the strange insistence on rejecting the use of English and the teaching of English, and even the intolerance of English usage by deaf persons capable of using it. There is a "NO VOICE" faction that seeks to prevent any teacher from using spoken English in class and to stop spoken English usage in general. Instead, all communication, including classroom instruction, would be limited to ASL. Never mind that there are no textbooks in ASL and that all textbooks are useless to those whose sole language is ASL.

As a result of this revolt, Gallaudet's current appointed president was chosen mostly for his deafness, not for any outstanding leadership or administrative abilities. His salary, paid by U.S. taxpayers, is among the highest of any university president in the country. Under his tutelage, Gallaudet has deteriorated apace, chiefly by his yielding to, perhaps condoning, changes seriously detrimental to the education of the students. Most blatant among these changes is the policy advocated by a group of extremists on the faculty of using ASL for all purposes, to the exclusion of all other means of communication, including other forms of signed or cued communication in English.

Indeed, in recent years, there has been a movement to get much of the teaching and communication to be via ASL only. Even the previously prevalent custom of teachers' speaking and signing simultaneously has been banned by this

# AN INTELLECTUAL LOOK AT ASL

"no-voice" policy, even outside the classroom and even with the hearing or oral deaf persons who rely on speech and speechreading. This is a clear violation of Section 104 of the Education of the Deaf Act as well as the ADA.

**Illiterate Gallaudet Graduates.** Gallaudet students and graduates -- including the very ones who plan to become teachers of the deaf -- are so abysmally lacking in minimal English language skills that most of them are unemployable in any setting other than residential schools for the deaf, and there only because such schools are notoriously unconcerned about such things.

Obviously any "University" whose graduates are only borderline literate is not deserving of the name to begin with, but to "market" such graduates *[Menzel is referring here to the Gallaudet University School of Education and Human Services]* as qualified teachers is preposterous. Accreditation of such a program by a responsible accrediting agency is unthinkable.

The extremists who have brought about these appalling conditions *[both at Gallaudet and at our residential schools for the deaf]* insist that deafness is not a disability at all, only a "cultural difference." (Parenthetically, this in no way dissuades them from applying for disability benefits through Social Security et al.) They insist that teachers of the deaf (many of whom are functionally illiterate themselves) do not need to pass a national test of English proficiency because such tests are discriminatory in view of the fact that the natural language of the deaf is ASL.

It is nothing new for Gallaudet to seek loopholes and circumvent the intent of Congress, but they are carrying it to new extremes. In summary, Gallaudet University is failing

# AN INTELLECTUAL LOOK AT ASL

abysmally to fulfill Congressional intent and its reasonable obligation to the public.

## VIOLATION OF PUBLIC LAW 94-142 IN OUR SCHOOLS FOR THE DEAF

Now we come to one of the most crucial violations of the letter and spirit of both the Education of the Deaf Act and the Individuals with Disabilities Education Act (IDEA): The exclusive use of ASL for all instruction is incompatible with the requirement under PL 94-142 that each handicapped child receive an education based on that child's individualized needs as determined through an interdisciplinary case study, culminating in an Individualized Education Program (IEP). There is obviously no way that any one educational approach will conform to the IEPs of all the children enrolled at residential schools for the deaf, especially in the Kendall Demonstration Elementary School and the Model Secondary School for the Deaf, both located on the campus of Gallaudet University.

## THE BILINGUAL-BICULTURAL MOVEMENT

Another coalition within the groups of ASL proponents is the "Bi-Bi" movement. The acronym stands for "Bilingual-Bicultural." This term is misleading, however. The "Bi-Bi" approach emphasizes teaching ASL (no English-based sign language, but strictly ASL) to the deaf child, intensively and extensively, until everyone is sure ASL has become his "first and native" language and he is thoroughly proficient in it. Then, and only then, English is introduced as a "second language," (by which is meant a secondary language) taught in the classroom using ASL as the language of instruction! Obviously this is done without textbooks, since ASL has no

# AN INTELLECTUAL LOOK AT ASL

written form and the child who has not yet learned English cannot read a textbook.

The rather substantial differences in grammar between ASL and English add considerably to the difficulty of using one in teaching the other. Despite the Bi-Bi advocates' insistence that ASL alone should be used, some variant based on English syntax would make the transition to English decidedly easier. Doing so would not detract from the value of using sign language.

Momentarily laying aside the central theme of this essay, the necessity of teaching English to deaf children, let it be said that the other misguided aim of the Bi-Bi advocates of using ASL as the language of instruction for all subjects is utterly harebrained. No weaker term will do. The learning of all academic subjects must depend heavily on textbooks and other printed material. The idea of trying to teach history or chemistry or math or civics or social studies through lectures signed in ASL alone flies in the face of all reason, and it takes more than fourth grade reading ability to grasp the subject matter in the textbooks.

A number of faculty members at Gallaudet -- by no means all -- are teaching via ASL exclusively, using no speech (not even mouthing), and preaching that ASL is sufficient for all communication needs of the deaf and that "Bi-Bi" is the way to teach in the primary and secondary schools for the deaf.

Using ASL to teach English to the deaf has never been proven to work. To the contrary, the Bi-Bi system tends to make children illiterate in two languages! *[Under the Bi-Bi system, a child is unable to read and write ASL, because ASL has no written form; therefore, he is illiterate in ASL. The child does not receive enough exposure and usage practice in*

# AN INTELLECTUAL LOOK AT ASL

*reading and writing English; consequently he is illiterate in English. As a result, the child is illiterate in two languages!]*

## AN UNWRITTEN LAW OF DEAF CULTURE

Although I would never claim that a hen is the best judge of a rotten egg, in order to understand the "deaf culture" it is necessary to see it through the eyes of an insider. That is not easy, owing to the unwritten law of the deaf culture that one never criticizes another member of it nor the deaf culture itself. This should not be surprising, in view of the fact that people so reared and so "educated" lack the necessary skills to be able to live successfully in the hearing society. Thus, the fear of ostracism from the only society they can function in keeps them silent, even if they harbor some disagreement.

This "rule of secrecy" that pervades the deaf culture, the overriding motive to cover up wrong-doing of all kinds, even at the risk of allowing serious crimes to go unpunished, is a tool that helps the cultists perpetuate themselves and their cult.

## MILITANT DEAF CHAUVINISTS

It was Napoleon who said: "There is no place in a fanatic's head where reason can enter." He could well have been thinking of the militant deaf chauvinists who stop at nothing in their incomprehensible determination to keep deaf infants deaf, to prevent deaf children from learning English and becoming literate, to preserve and intensify the isolation and insularity of the deaf and to fight against medical and technological advances geared toward overcoming deafness and its pernicious effects.

These extremists have a single purpose: The preservation and perpetuation of what they call "deaf culture."

# AN INTELLECTUAL LOOK AT ASL

This term by no means reflects an anthropologic phenomenon but, really, a cult rather than a culture. It is created for purely political purposes. In this age of rapid scientific, technologic and medical advancement, more and more congenital and early deafness is being prevented and better means devised for remediating, educating and habilitating deaf children. Some of those who have come to be recognized as "leaders" of the "deaf community" are fearful that the deaf community will dwindle to the point of no longer needing leaders.

Evidently then, the motive is preservation of their own status as leaders. Their enemy is assimilation of deaf children into the mainstream society through mastery of English and communication skills based on English. Hence their determination to prevent the acquisition of these skills and to keep deaf children isolated through absolute and exclusive dependence on American Sign Language and through enforced clannishness.

The one and only way to achieve the objectives of ASL advocates is through residential manual schools for the deaf, without which there would be no such thing as "deaf culture." Yet some of these very schools are said to be inherently harmful. There is a Dickensian cruelty to the children placed here by trusting parents who are far away and quite inaccessible to complaints by their offspring about cruelty, sexual abuse, educational ineptitude and much more. Neither has the child any other recourse. There is no "authority" to complain to except the very perpetrators of the inhumane treatment and their supervisors who invariably support the perpetrators. There is an incredible toleration of every kind of abuse within the school, including rape by staff and older students, inhuman and unwarranted "punishments," and of course inappropriate educational approaches.

# AN INTELLECTUAL LOOK AT ASL

Because of the low academic achievement levels required of residential students, the majority of graduates are on the Social Security Disability rolls and also receive Supplemental Security Income (SSI). Until those schools employ and support teachers who can and will teach deaf children English as well as other subjects, teachers who obviously have a good command of English themselves, and until they employ houseparents with professional attitudes and commensurate qualifications, and until the deaf children are given an education that enables them to obtain and hold jobs in some self-supporting line of work, the worst fears of the radical proponents of "deaf culture" will be realized *precisely because of their own misguided efforts to forestall the demise of "deaf culture."*

Parents of newly diagnosed deaf or hard of hearing children should assuredly read first-hand sources of information *[i.e.: "A Child Sacrificed to the Deaf Culture" and "No Dignity for Joshua" -- see inside back cover]* before they decide on the educational management of their children. This should especially take place before being exposed to the persuasion by the militant deaf leaders that *they* and not the parents should make all the decisions for the child, and that the deaf child in effect belongs to the deaf community and *not* its own parents.

## THE FEARS OF PROPONENTS OF DEAF CULTURE

When a writer recently quoted some of the angry reactions to a network TV program on cochlear implants, the words "child abuse" and "genocide" were surely most revealing as to the real motives of the extremists. They fear the demise of "deaf culture" unless a steady stream of new "recruits" can be maintained by preventing or discouraging parents of deaf

# AN INTELLECTUAL LOOK AT ASL

infants from either seeking remedies such as cochlear implants or placing their children in public or private schools where they can be "mainstreamed." In either case, such a child is apt to grow up as part of normal society, able to function and prosper in the hearing world. The radical deaf culturist finds that intolerable, as it is the residential schools for the deaf where all instruction is by sign language, particularly ASL, that are the breeding ground, the very marrow, of deaf culture.

This explains the motives of the leaders of the deaf community in opposing, nay fiercely fighting, any and every medical, social, or educational means of preventing or treating deafness in deaf children.

Suppose the "deaf culture" were really to become extinct for lack of unremediated, unrehabilitated new recruits. I have to ask: Can any sane person regret such an outcome?

## THE FATE OF MILITANT DEAF LEADERS AND DEAF CULTURE

There is no denying of course that it goes against fundamental American principles for any militant group to try to force other people to live as the militants tell them to. Such activities are by no means unique to the militant deaf "cultists," for we have long been plagued with fanatics trying to impose their beliefs on others.

I do perceive that their very militancy shows their fear of the inevitable demise of their cause, brought about by advances in medicine, technology, growing public recognition of the rights of people with disabilities and slowly growing enlightenment. The decline in enrollment at residential schools for the deaf has already forced some to close their doors and others will inevitably follow.

# AN INTELLECTUAL LOOK AT ASL

"Deaf culture" is doomed, for a combination of other reasons. As more and more genes that cause hereditary deafness are identified, it will become possible to identify their presence in the embryo and to treat the condition preventively. Continued improvements and expanded use of Cochlear Implants in young children will take many more out of the clutches of the chauvinists. For those that are left, there will be improved educational methods, more mainstreaming, better technology, speech-to-text devices built into eyeglasses, and lots more. People will wise up sooner or later. The radical ASL-only and Bi-Bi methods will die a natural death.

**CUED SPEECH: A RESURRECTION?**

The Cued Speech (CS) system has many virtues since being invented by Dr. R. Orin Cornett at Gallaudet University about thirty years ago. Aside from being easy to learn and effective in removing ambiguity from the spoken word, both receptively and expressively, it has been used very successfully in teaching deaf children language and speech, and appears to be generally far superior to the Bi-Bi approach that has had its ascendancy following the Gallaudet revolt in 1988.

Superficially, cueing looks somewhat like signing, but it is not a separate language from English. Instead, the handshapes, positions and movements supplement speechreading in a way so as to remove all ambiguity. A deaf person familiar with cued speech can follow every word that is spoken in English without the usual errors of interpretation. Morever, cued speech is easier to learn than ASL (in weeks rather than years) and is also a valuable tool for teaching speech to deaf children.

Dr. Cornett was Vice President at Gallaudet when he developed CS, and the system enjoyed considerable growth and respect at Gallaudet, which had a "Cued Speech Team" for years. However, because it appeared to bolster oralism, the hard core "Deaf Culture" chauvinists at Gallaudet managed to get the program abolished in 1995, with the acquiescence of their first deaf president who was chosen for his deafness, and assuredly not for his vision.

We need a new messiah to revive Cued Speech and restore it as a unique and valuable method both for educating deaf children and rehabilitating late deafened adults. I am of the opinion that the single best tool for teaching English to the deaf is Cued Speech, but parents and teachers must use it consistently and transliterators must be available.

**COCHLEAR IMPLANTS**

In the case of the Cochlear Implant (CI) for very young children, it is imperative for the child to receive intensive and extensive auditory training, speech and language training, lipreading training, and so forth. The implant combined with training -- and that means keeping it up for years, not just at the onset -- will make the great majority of these youngsters successfully oral, with good comprehension and good speech.

It is important to note that residential schools for the deaf are NOT the place for CI recipients. Culturally-deaf leaders have pointed out that in some residential schools one may find a few CI recipients who have not seemed to benefit from the device, singling them out as typical CI recipients. They disregard the fact that the lack of necessary auditory training, reinforcement and monitoring make the residential schools for the deaf themselves the *cause* of failure, not merely the witness to it!

# AN INTELLECTUAL LOOK AT ASL

## A STEP TOWARDS A DEAF SEXUAL ABUSE REMEDY

In a recent dual interview in *Hearing Health*, with National Association of the Deaf *[then]* President Benjamin Soukup and author Tom Bertling, Soukup wisely acknowledged that sexual abuse in residential schools does exist and that it is a serious problem. However, he stopped short of admitting the important point of Mr. Bertling's that administrators of those schools and others of the deaf community are doing nothing about it because they see it as something "normal." "We're used to it" is not an appropriate response. *[While solutions have proven to be somewhat elusive, irrefutable research evidence show that children ARE exposed to a dangerously high degree of risk at these residential schools. The overall lack of response from influential leaders of the deaf community is rather perplexing to those who are actively trying to reverse these conditions.]*

## CLOSING WORDS FOR PARENTS AND EDUCATORS

The most urgent need by far in educating the deaf child is to teach him English, not as a secondary language but as a primary language, coequally and concurrently with sign language, which may but need not be ASL. Whether or not he learns to speak, he must be helped to proficiency in reading, writing and comprehending English. Maximum exposure to English is essential, including the use of it in all instruction, whatever the school subject, and including an aggressive library program and encouragement to read for pleasure.

Proficiency in ASL is not an alternative to literacy! Fluency in English is neither a luxury nor an act of disloyalty to the deaf community; it is a necessity. The often repeated pronouncement by Gallaudet President I. King Jordan needs to

# AN INTELLECTUAL LOOK AT ASL

be amended to read: "Deaf people can do anything except hear, *provided they have a good working knowledge of the English language.*"

*[This essay was constructed and edited from the latest writings penned by Dr. Menzel prior to his untimely death. Many of these writings were published in numerous deafness-related periodicals, including a report to Congress. This essay also includes excerpts from his personal communication with the editor of this book. Reprinted with permission from Bettina B. Menzel.]*

"The Cued Speech team *[at Gallaudet]* was a victim of a crazy ASL cult juggernaut in 1995. They had the magic elixir in their hands and threw it away for a persimmon. When will they ever learn?"

"None are so deaf as those who will not listen."

"Proficiency in ASL is not an alternative to literacy."

"Let it be said that the misguided aim of the Bi-Bi advocates of using ASL as the language of instruction for all subjects is utterly harebrained. No weaker term will do."

*-Otto Menzel*

# AN INTELLECTUAL LOOK AT ASL

# CHAPTER THREE
## *THE ENGLISH ASPECT OF CURRICULUM FOR THE DEAF*
## *by Edward L. Scouten*

*[Edward Scouten is a retired distinguished educator of the deaf. A life-long advocate for English usage, he affiliated with several schools for the deaf as well as at Gallaudet University. In 1970, he was among the early educators at the newly founded National Technical Institute for the Deaf (NTID) located at the Rochester Institute of Technology where he remained until his retirement in 1986. It is our privilege to reprint this highly-regarded essay which also has been widely quoted.]*

### THE QUESTION OF NON-LANGUAGE SUBJECTS

A few years ago a brochure relative to a then upcoming conference on education of the deaf was widely circulated. In it were listed 12 educational areas from which interested persons could select topics for papers to be presented at the proposed conference.

I studied the topics carefully and was struck especially by one which was given under the heading of "instruction." This particular topic read as follows:

> *"Curriculum in academic (non-language) areas such as mathematics, science, social studies and the arts."*

Upon reading this, I was much amazed to find that the parenthetical adjective non-language was used to describe such

# AN INTELLECTUAL LOOK AT ASL

disciplines. How on earth could or should the subject of mathematics, which requires textbooks and the answering of language problems, be taught without reading and writing of English or any other orthographic language in which the subject might be presented? Again the same question might be asked relative to the teaching of science, social studies or the arts. Are these, too, to be considered non-language subjects? Even the arts involve language of some kind to express the terms of media, tools of work, and techniques. In fact, to consider the aforementioned subjects to be devoid of language, English, if you will, or any other language, is inconceivable.

## BARTLETT'S PRINCIPLE

David E. Bartlett epitomized the American tradition in education of the deaf when he wrote in 1852, "to educate the deaf . . . is to teach them language." It was adherence to this belief that made it possible to found Gallaudet College and subsequently many years later the National Technical Institute for the Deaf at RIT *[Rochester Institute of Technology]*.

Over the past 25 years, however, there has been a marked deviation from Bartlett's principle. The result of this deviation is reflected today in the average school for the deaf graduate's reading score which is somewhere at third or fourth grade level. Such a reading level is hardly a guarantee for the genuine success of any student entering college, let alone the hearing world of business, science and industry.

Today most collegiate faculties have come to believe that acceptable English achievement for prelingually deaf students is almost impossible. Consequently, there has been evolving over the years a quiet lessening of demands where written language requirements are concerned. Instead, there

# AN INTELLECTUAL LOOK AT ASL

has been an increasing emphasis placed on the more generic term *communication*.

## THE NATURE OF GESTURAL SYSTEMS

The term, *communication*, might be more specifically correct if modified to *gestural communication*, that is, the sending and receiving of ideas through gesticulation, facial expression and appropriate body movement. Through this unique mode, a world of ideas can be conveyed and received.

For any lay readers who may not be completely familiar with the American medium of gestural expression, we can illustrate by translating into gestures the English sentence, "I will go home tomorrow." First, this sentence may be translated into Signed English by substituting each English word with a corresponding gesture, thus preserving the English syntax. The fingerspelling of English words, however, is not necessary, excepting for proper names.

Next, in the American Sign Language (ASL), there are three possible translations for the sentence, "I will go home tomorrow." These variations are: (1) Me-home-tomorrow, (2) Home-tomorrow-me, and (3) Tomorrow-me-home. The virtue of ASL is not only its simplicity, but also its flexibility and economy of symbol.

## CURRENT EDUCATIONAL USE OF GESTURE

Unburdened with the complications of grammar and spelling as in English, Spanish, or Japanese, American Sign Language is quite undemanding intellectually. Therefore, it serves as a simple and quick mode of communication for deaf children. True to human nature, of course, they opt quite

# AN INTELLECTUAL LOOK AT ASL

naturally for this easy way to express themselves. Their acquisition of gesture is also greatly facilitated today through their observation and imitation of their teachers and dormitory houseparents *[at residential schools for the deaf]*. All this occurs, naturally, at the expense of valuable time which could be developed to usage-practice for English acquisition.

Most of the teachers do, however, supplement their gestures with English speech which provides a modicum of syntax for the children who can speechread and have some aural amplification. Many teachers, although they talk, still find that the abbreviated syntax of gestures is more readily understood. After all, the first objective which is urged upon them today is "communication."

## THE GROWING CRISIS IN ENGLISH ACQUISITION

As our linguistic expectations for prelingually deaf children have been lowered over the years, so in turn have our educational standards for them. The result is that we are today graduating young prelingually deaf people who are excellent in communicating *[using ASL]* with their teachers and with each other, but, unfortunately, they are hard put to read or write a straight English sentence.

How are these persons in the future to avail themselves of such modern linguistic advantages as the TDD, real-time graphic display, captioned films or closed-captions on television, if they are unable to read a simple note written on a piece of paper?

# AN INTELLECTUAL LOOK AT ASL

## A CONSIDERATION OF THE PAST FOR THE PRESENT PROBLEM

The language problem of prelingually deaf children is great, but certainly no greater than it was for the pupils of David E. Bartlett in 1852, or those pupils of Rochester's Z. F. Westervelt in 1878. Certainly, the language problem today is no greater than it was for the blind, deaf-mute pupil of Anne Sullivan *[Helen Keller]* in 1887. The genius of these early educators and others of their day lay in their mutual recognition of the fact that prelingually deaf children *could* learn English provided they were given:

1. Constant sensory exposure to the language to be learned.

2. Continuous opportunities for usage-practice of that language.

The denial of either of these two principles is sufficient to negate the entire language acquisition process. If we would extricate our deaf children of today from their language predicament, we, as educators, must rethink and revise our present instructional practices. If we wish to do this, it might be suggested that we emulate the efforts of the aforementioned eminent educators and others of the past. They have clearly marked the way for us to teach prelingually deaf children English or any other written language as a medium of thought and expression. Their recorded and empirically established precepts stand ready for the objective scrutiny of our modern linguistic and educational research, if such approval is necessary.

We do not need research, however, to tell us that reading and language classes *alone* are insufficient to provide

# AN INTELLECTUAL LOOK AT ASL

the average deaf child with enough usage-practice for him to acquire English as a practical medium of communication.

## A TOTAL SCHOOL COMMITMENT TO ENGLISH

The responsibility for language usage-practice must be shared by the teachers of all disciplines, both academic and vocational, as well as supportive services personnel and residential counselors. Parental support is also most crucial.

Accordingly, the teaching of a specialized vocabulary rests with a particular specialized teacher and so does the teaching of the correct syntactical usage of that specific vocabulary, be it relative to social studies, physical education, or auto body repair.

For too long our educational perspective has been dominated by a gestural surrogate *[ASL]* to the neglect of orthographic language, in our case, English, our language of business, science and industry.

## THE HEARING WORLD SETS THE REQUIREMENTS

Parents, not to mention other taxpayers, are all cognizant of the reading and writing of English as a basic requirement for the securing and holding of well paying jobs in the hearing world of work. Speech and aural amplification, both English based, will also facilitate the employment of our deaf youth in the hearing environment in which they will find themselves after graduation.

The hearing world is not to be down-played. It is an ever-present reality with which our prelingually deaf children and youth must learn to come to grips. They cannot successfully come to grips with this hearing world if they

# AN INTELLECTUAL LOOK AT ASL

cannot at least read and write adequately their own national language.

## ENGLISH, AN INTEGRAL PART OF EVERY DISCIPLINE

To sum up, all disciplines, both academic and non-academic, from preschool level through secondary, should be dedicated and coordinated to this *now* perceived "awesome task" of providing language acquisition for prelingually deaf children. Perhaps the task will become less awesome if educators will utilize *all* of their school facilities. For that first step, however, teachers must understand that the English aspect of curriculum is an integral part of every discipline. For deaf children and youth there are no non-language subjects.

## ADDENDUM: SOME ALMOST FORGOTTEN FACTS RECONSIDERED

In September, 1988 the National Conference on Deaf and Hard of Hearing People was held in El Paso, Texas. Numerous papers were presented. One paper with the very prosaic title "Current Employment Classification" was given by NTID's G.G. Walter and his colleague, J. MacLoed-Gallinger. Despite the title, the paper gave some very unprosaic information relative to the graduates of our schools for the deaf and their possibilities for success in postsecondary education. The first "jolt" was that . . . "only about 25 percent of the deaf persons beginning college will graduate . . ." (G.G. Walter, 1987)

The paper went on to say, "This high rate of attrition is probably a combination of lack of accommodation of the college environment to the special needs of deaf students and

# AN INTELLECTUAL LOOK AT ASL

relatively poor academic preparation of deaf high school graduates." (A footnote appears at this point) . . . "the median reading grade equivalent for 17-year-old hearing impaired students is 3.2 on the Stanford Achievement Tests *[Ed. note: SAT scores are indicated by grade level followed by the decimal fraction of the school year. Thus 3.2 would mean third-grade-level plus 1/5 or .2 of the school year.]*." (Allen, 1968)

> "As for the high school graduates who do not opt to attend college, their transition from high school to the world of work is likely to be extremely difficult . . . as evidenced by the large proportion of such graduates who are unemployed, and others who are neither in college nor in the labor force."

Another bit of information which should grab the attention of all teachers of deaf children and youth and particularly the attention of all school administrators is the observation that:

> ". . . we cannot lose the sight of the fact that collectively these young deaf adults continue to have measured achievement levels of fourth grade and below." (Allen, 1986)

By way of recommendation the investigators suggested that particular emphasis be given "to quality vocational training and placement" accompanied with " . . . a long term goal of increasing the overall achievement level, inclusively of literacy among deaf students graduating from high school." The final statement in the paper cogently advised that:

> " . . . we need to insure that high school students are prepared to enter the job market that expects sophistication in both technology and communication."

# AN INTELLECTUAL LOOK AT ASL

The word *communication* is interpreted by this writer to mean at least *the reading and writing of the English Language.*

Continuing in their conclusion, the authors of the paper stated that "the curricula of elementary, secondary, and post secondary programs must mount a unified effort to accommodate to the special needs of the deaf learner to ensure that graduates can attain their maximum potential."

The Walter and MacLoed-Gallinger paper was presented ten years ago. Since that revelation, few efforts have apparently been attempted to rectify this educational predicament at all levels of achievement. As Walter and MacLoed-Gallinger infer, this increase in English skills must start at the early learning levels if they are to produce effective results for deaf students upon graduation. If the English predicament continues to be ignored at the primary levels of learning, then this English language problem will jeopardize deaf students' future in postsecondary education, as well as their success in the workaday world.

Like most research in education of the deaf, this very pragmatic contribution appears to have been swept into oblivion, where a few school administrators probably will hope it will stay. Other administrators, however, with a little support and encouragement, may provide their prelingually deaf students with the opportunities afforded by practical English learning and usage environments.

Thus these students will be equipped to "enter a job market that expects sophistication both in technology and in communication." These two areas are essential for their success in the hearing world of work which inevitably awaits

# AN INTELLECTUAL LOOK AT ASL

them. Those prelingually deaf graduates who aspire to attend college will do so and will have at least a fighting chance for academic success.

Walter and MacLoed-Gallinger have, indeed, made a significant contribution to American education of the deaf in presenting this paper. The rest is up to us, all of us who are interested in the future of prelingually deaf people.

**REFERENCE:**
Walter, G.G. & MacLoed-Gallinger, J., "Current Employment, Demands and Opportunities: A Close Look at the Change." *The Proceedings of the National Conference on Deaf and Hard of Hearing People*, "Fort Monroe Revisited," El Paso, TX Sep. 13-18, 1988. pp.136-141.

*[Updated and reprinted with permission from Edward Scouten and the National Association of the Deaf.]*

". . . teachers must understand that the English aspect of curriculum is an integral part of every discipline. For deaf children and youth there are no non-language subjects."

"The hearing world is not to be down-played. It is an ever-present reality with which our prelingually deaf children and youth must learn to come to grips. They cannot successfully come to grips with this hearing world if they cannot at least read and write adequately their own national language."

*-Edward Scouten*

AN INTELLECTUAL LOOK AT ASL

# CHAPTER FOUR
## COCHLEAR IMPLANTS FOR YOUNG CHILDREN: ETHICAL ISSUES
### by Thomas Balkany, MD., Annelle V. Hodges, Ph.D., Kenneth W. Goodman, Ph.D.

*[This essay is an updated version of the authors' widely-quoted previous work on the motives of the leaders of Deaf culture. While they write from the perspective of being advocates for the rights of deaf children, this essay provides revealing and indispensable information for all educators, administrators and professionals for the deaf as well as parents of deaf children and their families. Dr. Balkany is the Hotchkiss Professor and Vice Chairman of the University of Miami Ear Institute., Dr. Hodges is an Assistant Professor and Chief of Audiology. Dr. Goodman is the Director of the Forum for Bioethics and Philosophy. All are at the U. of Miami.]*

Ethics is the study of such concepts as goodness, duty, rightness and obligation. In bioethics, these concepts are applied to practical problems raised in health care and biomedical research. Many of these problems arise along with the testing and adoption of new medical technologies. The second half of the 20th century has seen an extraordinary array of new and evolving technologies, ranging from organ transplantation and gene manipulation to life support systems and electronic medical records. This chapter considers ethical

# AN INTELLECTUAL LOOK AT ASL

controversy surrounding another technological development: cochlear implants for children, and is based in part on the authors' previous work in this area (Balkany, Hodges, & Goodman, 1996).

Cochlear implants (CIs) represent an emerging technology that has the potential to change fundamentally the way people live. From the medical point of view, the CI is a safe and effective treatment for a severe disability -- profound deafness. From the point of view of Deaf culture, however, it is unnecessary technology that is demeaning to deaf people's way of life (Lane, 1993). In the opinion of some Deaf activists, *[virtually all ASL advocates are also advocates for Deaf culture]* anything that prevents deafness or restores hearing to children who are deaf, threatens Deaf society (Lane, 1993; Pollard, 1987). As a result of this perceived threat, there have been organized attempts to suppress CIs throughout the 1990s (Balkany, 1993).

It is essential to appreciate that Deaf society is dependent for perpetuation of itself on children who are deaf and whose parents have normal hearing. Since 90 percent of children who are deaf are born to two hearing parents and 97 percent to at least one hearing parent, it is widely thought that if parents were given a safe and effective option to provide hearing to their child, many would choose to do so. If a large number of children who are deaf did not enter Deaf society, that society could be essentially changed. And because medical technology affects society, conflicts of an ethical nature may occur.

Members of mainstream society, or even the blind (who share with the deaf the inability to utilize one of humankind's dominant senses, but may not otherwise be similar), may have difficulties understanding opposition to providing a child who

# AN INTELLECTUAL LOOK AT ASL

is deaf with the ability to hear. However, many in the Deaf community see their way of life as emotionally fulfilling, promising, and independent without hearing (Balkany, 1993; Balkany & Hodges, 1995: Balkany, 1995). Some Deaf leaders also claim that the deaf are an oppressed linguistic minority and that any intervention to provide hearing to children who are deaf is inherently racist (Lane, 1993).

In the case of cochlear implants for children, the elements of conflict may be framed as issues that concern honesty, autonomy, beneficence, the best interests of the child, the needs of a linguistic minority to perpetuate itself, the cost of deafness to society, and acceptance of diversity.

**TRUTHFULNESS**

It is inherent that CI teams recommending implantation truthfully provide full information to parents as part of the process of obtaining informed consent. This includes not only describing the risks and benefits of the operation, but also ensuring that parents understand the limitations of the technology, the requirement for auditory (re)habilitation, as well as the options of joining Deaf society, communicating in American Sign Language (ASL), and avoiding "treatment" of deafness entirely.

Deaf culture is rich and diverse, and its members are bonded by ASL as well as by social and political organizations (Balkany, 1993; Lane, Hoffmeister, & Bahan, 1996). Deaf people attend parties, date, marry, have families, and raise children. In short, there are many positive aspects of life in the Deaf community, and they are best described to parents by a member of Deaf society.

Just as CI teams do with CIs, Deaf society proponents have an inherent responsibility to describe fully the positive as

# AN INTELLECTUAL LOOK AT ASL

well as the negative aspects of life in Deaf society and to state their reasons for opposition to restoration of hearing. As in the informed-consent process for surgery, this discussion needs to be truthful and complete, allowing parents the autonomy to decide for themselves whether their child should receive a CI. Unfortunately, many members of Deaf society have been misinformed about CIs. One reason this has occurred is that the average graduate of a Deaf residential high school reads at a third- to fourth-grade level (Dolnick, 1993; Conrad, 1979) and is thus incapable of accessing moderately sophisticated published information in the lay media. Since there is no written form of ASL, many in the Deaf community rely on informal sources of information such as newsletters and storytellers at Deaf clubs. Deaf leaders and educators who, to a substantial degree, control this information, have misled the Deaf community in a highly successful effort to generate opposition to CIs (Balkany, 1995).

Examples of the misleading, pejorative picture of CIs painted by Deaf leaders include articles in Deaf culture newsletters:

"I would be remiss not to equate cochlear implants with genocide" (Silver, 1992).

"There is absolutely no question that our government has a hidden agenda for deaf children much akin to Nazi experiments on Holocaust victims" (Silver, 1992).

"Using deaf children as 'lab rats' and medical guinea pigs is profoundly disturbing" (Roots, 1994).

Much more distressing, however, are inventions by respected colleagues designed to sway public opinion. Dr. Yerker Andersson, Professor and Chairman, Department of Deaf Studies at Gallaudet University and Emeritus President of the World Federation of the Deaf, published an article in the

# AN INTELLECTUAL LOOK AT ASL

*World Federation of the Deaf News* in which he reported (without supporting reference) a surgeon who was "eager to use his skills on 17 Deaf individuals." According to Prof. Andersson, "Three died due to complications and one became mentally ill. The rest were failures" (Andersson, 1994). In fact, no deaths or cases of mental illness have been caused by CIs, and after hundreds of scientific papers and years of study, the U.S. Federal Drug Administration, medical oversight organizations, and even insurance carriers have concluded that CIs are safe and effective (Balkany, 1993). To say simply that Andersson was incorrect is to underestimate his scholarly abilities.

It is generally considered unethical to mislead people purposefully in order to persuade them to a point of view. The ethical principle violated by Andersson and others is autonomy as it relates to self-determination. People are deprived of their right to decide for themselves when they have been purposefully misled.

It is not surprising that, as a result of widespread misinformation, there is widespread misunderstanding. Many people who are deaf fervently believe that CIs are often fatal or severely damaging to children and they are therefore opposed to them. The following are representative verbatim quotations from the future leaders of the Deaf community, college students at Gallaudet:

"I read few articles about how cochlear implant. For deaf people died from cochlear implant. It was explained about how cochlear implant affected to brain damage."

"I feel that cochlear implants are wrong because it makes the recipient a robot with wires sticking out of their head."

"I may not aware of cochlear implant much but I do have a strong against it" (letters to the William House Cochlear Implant

# AN INTELLECTUAL LOOK AT ASL

Study Group, a committee of the American Academy of Otolaryngology -- Head and Neck Surgery, 1993; author's files).

**INTERNAL INCONSISTENCY AND CONFLICT OF INTEREST**

Other examples of failure to respect the value of truthfulness are seen in Deaf leaders' advocacy of mutually contradictory positions. For example, it is claimed that deafness is not a disability and, at the same time, that people who are deaf are entitled to disability benefits amounting to billions of dollars per year. Another is that CIs do not work and also that they work so well as to eliminate deafness (genocide). Consciously supporting both sides of mutually exclusive arguments in order to influence public opinion is not considered ethical behavior. Deaf advocates must decide whether to tell parents that the deaf or hard of hearing are independent or that the majority require disability (and other entitlement) benefits. They must decide whether it is ethical to say to parents that CIs don't work and to politicians that CIs work so well that they are genocidal.

Deaf activists who believe that their way of life is threatened by CIs may find themselves in conflict of interest. Barbara White, writing as an Associate Professor at Gallaudet, succinctly reveals this conflict of interest: ". . . the future of the deaf community is at stake. An entire subculture of America will no longer exist" (letters to the William House Cochlear Implant Study Group, a committee of the American Academy of Otolaryngology - Head and Neck Surgery, 1993; author's files). (Ear surgeons may be at similar risk for conflict of interest. It is estimated that CI surgery, however, constitutes less than one-tenth of one percent of the operations performed by otologists. A CI program, rather than generating income,

# AN INTELLECTUAL LOOK AT ASL

actually costs a great deal to sustain by cost shifting and philanthropy.)

This potential conflict of interest among members of the Deaf community may operate to the disadvantage of individual children who are deaf. Australian physician Henley Harrison wrote, "The motive in opposing cochlear implants in children is self-interest rather than the children's welfare. . . it is the welfare of the children that should be borne in mind, not some other group" (Harrison, 1991).

Ethical standards hold that Deaf advocates should reveal such conflicts of interest to parents who are considering the merits of life in Deaf society for their children. As a three-generation member of the Deaf community warns, "Parents should cast a cautious eye towards anyone wanting to sacrifice a deaf child towards preserving a culture" (Bertling, 1994).

In short, representatives of the Deaf community who wish to influence parents and the public must begin truthfully to reveal both the advantages and the disadvantages of life in Deaf society. Only in this way can parents make an informed decision regarding the best interests of their child.

**IS DEAFNESS A DISABILITY?**

Examination of the position that deafness constitutes neither a handicap nor a disability, but only an oppressed linguistic minority (Lane et al., 1996) is a central issue in the discourse about CIs for children. Deaf leaders surely understand that if deafness is not a disability, people who are deaf or hard of hearing must give up billions of dollars in public assistance that is intended for the disabled. In writing from the ethical perspective, Englehardt (1986) defines disability as the failure to achieve an expected state of function. Boorse (1975) more precisely defines disability as occurring

# AN INTELLECTUAL LOOK AT ASL

(a) when a specific function is impaired, (b) there is reduced ability below typical efficiency, or (c) a limitation of functional ability occurs with reference to the patient's age or gender group.

It is clear that, in addition to its cultural definition, deafness fits the functional definition of a disability; but how does it compare with other disabilities? According to a California Department of Rehabilitation survey published in 1993, in which clients with all types of disabilities filled out self-assessment forms, deafness was associated with the lowest educational level, the lowest family income, the lowest percentage working, the lowest percentage in professional/technical jobs, and the poorest *self-assessment* of well-being (Harris, Anderson, & Novak, 1995). This study suggests that deafness is not only a disability, but that it may be among the most disabling of disabilities.

To deny that deafness is a disability, Deaf leaders must also deny its cost to society: $377,000 per child in K-12 residential Deaf school education (estimated $121.8 billion for educating all people who are deaf or hard of hearing at residential schools), $2.5 billion per year in lost workforce productivity, and more than $2 billion annually for the cost of equal access, Social Security Disability Income, Medicare, and other entitlements of the disabled (National Institutes of Health, 1992). As Tom Bertling, a third-generation member of Deaf culture, notes in his book, *A Child Sacrificed*, "Virtually every aspect of the deaf community is dependent on government support for the disabled" (Bertling, 1994).

Perhaps the greatest monetary cost to society of the disability of deafness is in education. It is estimated that the cost of kindergarten through 12th-grade education in Rhode Island is about $9,000 per hearing child. For children who are

# AN INTELLECTUAL LOOK AT ASL

deaf who are mainstreamed in public schools, the cost jumps to $44,000 per child. If the same deaf students attend residential schools for the Deaf, the cost becomes $429,000 per child (Johnson, Mauk, Takeawa, Simon, et al., 1993).

At this high cost, what are the outcomes of current methods of, and approaches to educating students who are deaf or hard of hearing? The average reading level of an adult who is deaf is at third or fourth grade (Conrad, 1979); further, when students who are deaf or hard of hearing finish high school, three out of four cannot read a newspaper (Dolinick, 1993). In large part because of this low educational outcome, the deaf are too often unemployed or underemployed, resulting in a cost to society of $2.5 billion per year in lost wages (National Institutes of Health, 1992).

The Deaf community is well aware of the rights of the disabled under the Americans with Disabilities Act. As an example, a woman who was deaf sued a Maryland volunteer fire department because she was not selected to be a fire fighter (Strom, 1994). She was, presumably, unable to hear sirens, alarms, calls for help, or instructions for emergency action, and she could not express her own needs or instructions with sign language while holding a fire hose or climbing a ladder.

A controversial risk of deafness that is rarely discussed with parents is the prevalence of psychological disorders. Although this relationship has been confirmed by hundreds of independent investigators and scientific papers, the data on morbidity have been attributed by Deaf leaders both to poor parenting and to culturally/linguistically biased testing (Lane, 1993). Debate over the value of such data notwithstanding, ethical representatives of Deaf society must decide whether it

# AN INTELLECTUAL LOOK AT ASL

is appropriate to discuss these studies with parents whom they are counseling about life in Deaf culture.

Another area that remains obscured from parents is much more difficult to approach delicately. Tom Bertling, in his second book, *No Dignity for Joshua* (1997), describes in painful detail the ongoing problem with the physical, emotional, and sexual abuse that occurs, especially to very young children, in residential Deaf schools. He feels that abuse is widespread, owing to a combination of low salaries paid to the nonprofessional members of the staff at state-run Deaf schools, a tendency among the Deaf community to conceal internal affairs, quasi-acceptance of such behavior within Deaf culture, and difficult communication between parents and their children who use ASL. Bertling's experiences are supported by scientific studies of over 480 abused children by Sullivan and colleagues (Sullivan, Brookhouser, Scanlan, Knutson, et al., 1991) showing a high incidence of sexual abuse in residential Deaf schools. On the basis of this awareness, several states are interceding to provide better supervision, especially for children who are deaf under the age of five years (Bertling, 1994). Although similar problems may also occur at any residential school where poorly trained staff are underpaid, Deaf advocates must decide whether the ethical principle of truthfulness requires that parents be made aware of possible problems of sexual and other abuse at residential Deaf schools.

## DEAF LEADERS VS. PARENTS

Deaf activists hold conferences on the unseemly topic, "Who Owns the Deaf Child?" (Barringer, 1993). Their answer is that children who are deaf or hard of hearing are de facto members of the Deaf community and that hearing parents are

# AN INTELLECTUAL LOOK AT ASL

obliged to "give up the child" (a phrase used by the Deaf) to be acculturated by Deaf society (Dolnick, 1993). By this, Deaf activists mean that the usual values taught in families, including morals, ethics, religion, love, security, self-esteem, as well as language, should be taught by culturally Deaf adults who are not part of the child's family (Lane, 1993). This process is termed *horizontal acculturation* (as opposed to *vertical acculturation*, in which these values are taught by parent to child, generation after generation). They claim horizontal acculturation is best accomplished by removing the child from the home and placing him or her in a residential Deaf school (Lane, 1993).

Dr. Marina McIntire, director of ASL programs at Northeastern University, notes, "It has been argued that hearing parents have 'the right' to raise youngsters who are linguistically and culturally like themselves. We disagree" (letters to the William House Cochlear Implant Study Group, a committee of the American Academy of Otolaryngology -- Head and Neck Surgery, 1993; author's files). Roz Rosen, then president of the U.S. National Association of the Deaf in 1992, now the vice president of Academic Affairs at Gallaudet University, concurs: "Hearing parents are not qualified to decide about implants" (Coffey, 1992). In his book, *The Mask of Benevolence*, Dr. Harlan Lane states that parents cannot make decisions for their own child who is deaf because they don't "really know the patient" and are in a "conflict of interest with their own child." Lane has previously taken the position that a culturally Deaf adult who is not related to the child should be empowered to override the child's parents and make the decision as to whether a child should receive a CI (Lane, 1993).

# AN INTELLECTUAL LOOK AT ASL

This proposed intrusion into the American family is in direct conflict with Public Laws 94-142 and 99-4457, which ensure that children who are deaf are educated in the least restrictive environment (i.e., most like nonhandicapped children). These laws empower families of deaf children, and are directly opposed to horizontal acculturation (Gearhart, Wright, 1979; Katz, Marthis, & Merril, 1978).

## IMPORTANT QUESTIONS

Thus, two important questions arise regarding CIs for children: (1) Who should decide for the child? and (2) According to what standards should the decision be made?

The courts, as well as legal scholars and ethicists, concur that the rights and concerns of self-interest groups should be strictly excluded from decisions concerning the well-being of individual children (Buchanan & Brock, 1989). Interference from outside groups deprives families of their right to privacy. As Buchanan and Brock (1989) state in their book, *Deciding for Others: The Ethics of Surrogate Decision Making*, "the family must have great freedom from oversight, control and intrusion to make important decisions about the welfare of its children. Society should be reluctant to intercede in a family's decision." Parents exercise free informed consent on behalf of their children. "Others do not have the right to intervene in their . . . actions" (Englehardt, 1986).

In addition, "There must be a clear locus of authority or decision making will lack coherence, continuity and accountability" (Buchanan & Brock, 1989). Only the child's parents, or in their absence, a legal guardian who has authority for all aspects of the child's life, can provide such continuity and accountability. The suggestion that a culturally Deaf individual be appointed to decide whether a child should or

# AN INTELLECTUAL LOOK AT ASL

should not receive a CI (or, for that matter, any other medical treatment or procedure) would violate the principle of a clear locus of authority because that individual would not have authority or responsibility for any aspect of the child's life.

However, parental rights to make health care decisions for children, while broad, are not unlimited. For instance, a decision to forgo treatment for a disability or other treatable disorder might appropriately be regarded as neglect. Nonetheless, the exercise of a parent's judgment is rarely constrained, and only in extreme cases of neglect is parental judgment overridden.

Parents must bear the consequences and are financially responsible for decisions made about their children. Thus, only parents can decide for the child. But according to what principles should the choice be made?

## AUTONOMY AND BENEFICENCE

Buchanan and Brock (1989) identify two underlying ethical values in making decisions for others: respect for self-determination (autonomy) and concern for well-being (beneficence).

In foreseeing the desire of special-interest groups such as Deaf society for influence, Engelhardt (1986) states, "This principle of autonomy provides moral grounding for public policies aimed at defending the innocent." In exercising autonomy for their children, parents act within the rights of their children, which include freedom of choice, respect for the individual, and free, informed consent to make decisions on behalf of their child. Engelhardt (1986) defines free choices as "being unrestrained by prior commitments or justified authority, and being free from coercion."

# AN INTELLECTUAL LOOK AT ASL

Associated with the right to self-determination is the right to privacy. When Deaf activists attempt to impose their wishes on parents of deaf children and suggest that parents are in conflict of interest with their own children, that they are not aware of their own children's best interests, and that only culturally Deaf adults should be allowed to act as proxy decision makers on behalf of the deaf child (Lane, 1993), they ignore the family's right to privacy and self-determination and, in doing so, trample the family's autonomy.

The ethical value of beneficence also guides parents. In simplest terms, it involves a prudent effort to do good and avoid evil (Englehardt, 1986). Advocates of Deaf culture who claim that making CIs available to children who are deaf is tantamount to "genocide" for Deaf culture are more concerned with doing good and avoiding evil to their culture than honoring the value of beneficence as it applies to the child.

Beneficence also applies to the child's "right to an open future" (Buchanan & Brock, 1989). Children have clear interest in maintaining and developing functional abilities. The ability to hear not only is communicative value but also provides auditory enjoyment and is important to safety. Children who are deaf or hard of hearing also have an "opportunity interest" regarding preservation of opportunity for their future education, employment and interpersonal relationships. Educational and employment expectations for culturally Deaf persons are unfortunately lower than those for hearing people (Balkany & Hodges, 1995; Dolnick, 1993). Since 99.8 percent of the population of the United States cannot communicate in ASL (Padden, 1987), opportunities for personal relationships (teachers, bus drivers, neighbors, friends) are highly restricted by primary or sole communication in ASL. Conversely, entering the hearing world may increase

# AN INTELLECTUAL LOOK AT ASL

opportunity for education, employment, and personal relationships.

## STANDARDS FOR MAKING SURROGATE DECISIONS

In addition to the two ethical values mentioned, there are three well-established standards for making surrogate decisions: advance directive, substituted judgment, and best interest. If an advance directive has been established by the patient, such as a living will or a specific nomination of surrogate, it should be meticulously followed. If none is available, a family member should make decisions on the basis of substituted judgment (using knowledge of the person, the surrogate does what he or she believes the person would do under the circumstances, if the person were competent). Neither of these first two standards applies to children. The third guiding standard, which does apply to children, is that of best interest. It is the parents' responsibility to make decisions according to their understanding of what is in the best interest of their child.

## DIVERSITY

A possible solution to the ethical conflict between the child's best interest and the needs of Deaf society to perpetuate itself lies in the well-established principle of social diversity. Efforts by Deaf leaders to keep the Deaf community pure, however, systematically exclude people who may be slightly different, for example, children who are deaf or hard of hearing and who have CIs. This demand for cultural purity, and the attendant exclusionary behavior, is generally not tolerated in advanced societies.

# AN INTELLECTUAL LOOK AT ASL

Diversity is a valued strength of modern society that requires open-mindedness and fairness. Whereas Deaf leaders rightfully insist that mainstream society accept Deaf persons, Deaf society itself systematically excludes children who are deaf or hard of hearing and who use CIs. As Bienvenu and Colonomos state, ". . . implanted children can never be fully accepted within the Deaf community" (letters to the William House Cochlear Implant Study Group, a committee of the American Academy of Otolaryngology -- Head and Neck Surgery, 1993; author's files). Lane (1993) agrees that if CI patients "turn to the deaf community for support, they experience discrimination." Donnel Ashmore states that "if a child shows 'signs of hearism' this will result in a hostile, silent reprimand" (Lane, 1993)

CI recipients in elementary schools have recently been taught a new sign for CIs by adult interpreters for the Deaf: the sign for "snake bite" made behind the ear. Such stigmatization is typical of societies that attempt to keep their ranks "pure" and avoid diversity.

Deaf advocates who oppose the diversity that children with CIs might bring seem to ignore the fact that the Deaf community is already diverse -- socially, economically, educationally, and politically. Welcoming children who are deaf or hard of hearing and who are "different" (because they can use the CI to help them communicate) to be part of their community may enlarge and strengthen Deaf society.

## CHANGING WITH THE TIMES

Two recent strategic shifts in position have been notable in opposition to CIs: (a) In view of data showing remarkable hearing and language acquisition by children with CIs, some leaders have stopped emphasizing that CIs don't

# AN INTELLECTUAL LOOK AT ASL

work and have begun to promote the notion that even if CIs restored hearing perfectly, they would be unacceptable (Lane, 1993); and (b) Many Deaf leaders have retreated from their arguments that a representative of Deaf culture must decide whether a child receives a CI. They now agree that parents be allowed that choice (Lane et al., 1996). It is hoped that others will follow this logic.

Another recent position adopted by some Deaf leaders is that cochlear implant professionals are in violation of United Nations conventions proscribing limitation of the growth of linguistic minorities. It would follow that since CIs work, they would limit the growth of the Deaf community (a linguistic minority). Therefore, CIs are forbidden by the United Nations. This line of reasoning clearly establishes that these leaders are more concerned with the needs of their culture than with the best interests of deaf children.

In summary, the term deafness describes both an important, respected way of life and a disability. The ethical standard of truthfulness requires that representatives of Deaf society inform parents of both the positive and the negative qualities of life in Deaf society and that CI teams do the same regarding CIs.

The ethical values of autonomy and beneficence and the need for a single locus of authority in raising children determine that *parents* decide whether their child should receive a CI. The guiding standard for such a surrogate decision is best interest. Thus, parents must determine what is in the best interest of their child. The need of Deaf Society to perpetuate itself has no bearing on that decision, although parents should consider the opinions and experiences of truthful Deaf adults.

# AN INTELLECTUAL LOOK AT ASL

The Deaf community should demand the same acceptance of diversity from itself that it does from mainstream society. There must be room for all who wish to join. Deaf society's goal of ethnic purity and its exercise of discriminatory exclusion of deaf children who have CIs countervail the norms of ethical behavior and weaken its moral position.

**REFERENCES:**

Andersson, Y. (1994). Do we want cochlear implants? *World Federation of the Deaf News, 1,* 3-4.

Balkany, T. (1993). A brief perspective on cochlear implants. *New England Journal of Medicine, 328,* 281-282.

Balkany, T. (1995). The rescuers, cochlear implants: Habilitation or genocide? *Advances on Otorhinolaryngology, 50,* 4-8.

Balkany, T., & Hodges, A.V. (1995). Misleading the deaf community about cochlear implantation in children. *Annals of Otolaryngology, 104* (Suppl. 116), 148-149.

Balkany, T., Hodges, A.V., & Goodman, K.W. (1996) Ethics of cochlear implantation in young children. *Archives of Otolaryngology--Head & Neck Surgery, 144,* 748-755.

Barringer, F. (1993, May 16). Pride in a soundless world. *New York Times* (pp. 1, 14).

Bertling, T. (1994). *A child sacrificed to the deaf culture.* Wilsonville, OR: Kodiak Media Group.

Bertling, T. (1997). *No dignity for Joshua.* Wilsonville, OR: Kodiak Media Group.

Boorse, C. (1975). On the distinction between disease and illness. *Philosophy and Public Affairs, 5,* 61.

Buchanan, A.E., & Brock, D.W. (1989). *Deciding for others. The ethics of surrogate decision making.* Cambridge, MA: Cambridge University Press.

Coffey, R. (1992). Caitlin's story on "60 Minutes." *The Bicultural Center News, 53,* 3.

Conrad, R. (1979). *The deaf school child: Language and cognitive function.* New York: Harper & Row.

Dolnick, E. (1993, September). Deafness as culture. *The Atlantic Monthly,* 37-53.

# AN INTELLECTUAL LOOK AT ASL

Englehardt, H.T. (1986). *The foundation of bioethics*. New York: Oxford University Press.

Gearhart, B.R., & Wright, W.S. (1979). *Organization and administration of educational programs for exceptional children*. Springfield, IL: Charles C. Thomas.

Harris, J.P., Anderson, J.P., & Novak, R. (1995). An outcome study of cochlear implants in deaf patients. *Archives of Otolaryngology--Head & Neck Surgery, 121,* 398-404.

Harrison, H.C. (1991). Deafness in children. *Medical Journal of Australia, 154,* 11.

Johnson, J.L., Mauk, G.W., Takekawa, K.M., Simon, P.R., et al. (1993). Implementing a statewide system of services for infants with hearing disabilities. *Seminars in Hearing, 14,* 105-118.

Katz, L., Marthis, S.L., & Merril, E.C. (1978). *The deaf child in the public schools*. Danville, IL: Interstate Printers.

Lane, H. (1993) *Mask of benevolence*. New York: Vintage Books.

Lane, H., Hoffmeister, R., & Bahan, B. (1996). *A journey into the deaf world*. San Diego, CA: Dawn Sign Press.

National Institutes of Health Consensus Statement. (1992). *Early identification of hearing impairment in infants and young children, 11* (1), 1-12.

Padden, C.A. (1987) American Sign Language. In *Gallaudet encyclopedia of deaf people and deafness* (Vol. 3, pp. 43-53). Washington, DC: Gallaudet University Press.

Pollard, R.Q. (1987) Cross cultural ethics in the conduct of deafness research. *Rehabilitation Psychology, 37,* 87-99.

Roots, J. (1994). Deaf Canadian fighting back. *World Federation of the Deaf News,* 2-3.

Silver, A. (1992). Cochlear implant: Surefire prescription for long-term disaster. *TBC News, 53,* 4-5.

Strom, K.E. (1994, February). Disability regulations review. *Hearing Review,* 12-14.

Sullivan, P.M., Brookhouser, P.E., Scanlan, J.M., Knutson, J.F., et al. (1991). Patterns of physical and sexual abuse of communicatively handicapped children. *Annals of Otology, Rhinology & Laryngology, 100,* 188-194.

# AN INTELLECTUAL LOOK AT ASL

*[This essay was first printed in the book titled: "CIs for Kids," Warren Estabrooks, Editor, and published in 1998 by The Alexander Graham Bell Association for the Deaf in Washington, D.C. Reprinted with permission from Dr. Thomas Balkany and Warren Estabrooks.]*

"Just as CI teams do with CIs, Deaf society proponents have an inherent responsibility to describe fully the positive as well as the negative aspects of life in Deaf society and to state their reasons for opposition to restoration of hearing."

*- Balkany et al.*

# AN INTELLECTUAL LOOK AT ASL

# CHAPTER FIVE

## *STATE RESIDENTIAL SCHOOLS FOR THE DEAF: A NEW ROLE?*
## *by Tom Bertling*

**HISTORICAL TRUTHS, (AND MISTRUTHS) ABOUT RESIDENTIAL SCHOOLS**

Any discussion about residential schools for the deaf should begin with a historical perspective for complete understanding of what these schools or institutions are really supposed to be.

To begin with, early in the 19th century, the deaf and other "uneducables" were placed into institutions or asylums for partial education and vocational training. These institutions were not considered academic schools. The majority of deaf children ended up in one of these since the alternative then usually meant no education at all. However, those succeeding with the oral method were rarely placed in one. As hearing aid technology improved, many hard-of-hearing children were mainstreamed into fully academic education, leaving the institutions mostly with the severely and profoundly (usually prelingually) deaf children. An increasing number of deaf children, falling within this latter category, gradually found themselves mainstreamed when signs based on English-word-order and the more recent Cued Speech came into being.

# AN INTELLECTUAL LOOK AT ASL

As a result, in recent years, these institutions have ended up with more and more deaf children who have additional problems such as mental retardation, learning disabilities and other defects that make them "functionally uneducable" in mainstream settings. Researchers studying these things remind us that this is exactly why these schools were created and funded by the states in the first place -- a place for the "functionally uneducable."

As technology and increasing numbers of methods of educating the deaf evolved, deaf children are finding their way out of these institutions with many never being sent to one. In many European countries, like Great Britain, deaf children in residential schools that can be academically educated are kept separate from those having additional disabilities or behavior problems. These two groups are never mixed as they are in present-day American residential institutions for the deaf.

For anyone to believe *today* that these "schools" in America are the ideal place to send the average deaf child is to be completely ignorant about deaf education. For school administrators of these residential schools to continue misleading parents is perhaps the most serious ethical infringement of the trust parents have placed in our school administrators and educators.

Sadly today, for whatever reasons, our residential schools are still filled with otherwise intelligent deaf children who are living and learning "side-by-side" with truly "functionally uneducable" deaf children. The previous practice in residential schools of placing less abled students in "special classes" is gradually being discontinued. Long-term educators of the deaf have pointed out that this "side-by-side" situation is becoming more possible through the use of ASL which

# AN INTELLECTUAL LOOK AT ASL

forms a commonality for learning and communication. However, that "commonality" is mutual English illiteracy.

## THREE MAJOR PROBLEM AREAS PLAGUING RESIDENTIAL SCHOOLS

Most knowledgeable people today will agree that there are three major problem areas plaguing our state residential schools for the deaf. The same also argue these schools are having varying degrees of difficulty overcoming the problems confronting them.

One is the notoriously low educational output that has historically tormented these residential schools. Researchers are reminding us that since these schools were intended for the "functionally uneducable," full academic learning was never part of the design. Others associated with them have noted that efforts over the years to produce full academic programs have plateaued and are now on the downward swing. Although proponents of these schools have been rather expedient in the assignment of blame for these poor conditions, the fact of the matter is the average prelingually-, profoundly-deaf graduate of these schools still cannot read and write in English beyond approximately the 4th grade level, and, in many cases, the 2nd grade level.

The second area of concern is the cost to society. The cost of educating a deaf child at a residential school for the deaf is multiplied by a factor of ten compared to educating the same child in a mainstream program *[see Balkany et al.]*. Without a doubt, we are not seeing a corresponding ratio in educational outcomes. In fact, even with the tenfold additional funds they still cannot bring the level of facilities, equipment, standards and quality of staffing up to what is available in mainstream schools. Many will (rightly) argue that

# AN INTELLECTUAL LOOK AT ASL

a deaf child receives *both* a far superior education *and* a far superior educational experience in mainstream programs.

The third major area of concern is the recent disclosure that sexual, mental and emotional abuse have also historically plagued these schools. This problem has proven to be rather difficult to resolve and it has gone so far that in one state (Virginia) the legislators literally suggested closing the residential school to get out of the sex policing business after earlier attempts by the school administrators failed to reverse sexual abuse occurrences. While it is true that sexual abuse occurs nearly everywhere in our society, most parents are unaware of these occurrences and leaders of the deaf have done next to nothing to help resolve these problems. In fact, many of them are guilty of deliberately withholding this information from parents. As this book went to press, numerous newspaper headlines detailing these sexual abuse problems suggest both these problems are still occurring and that a solution is nowhere in sight. *[See the author's book "No Dignity for Joshua" for further details.]*

That all three problems continue to be unresolved, requires some action expedient to their solution. We cannot allow these residential school administrators to continue to mislead parents of deaf children, claiming that their institutions are better than the alternatives. These administrators, influenced by ASL advocates and activists of the Bi-Bi theory, started using the reasoning of "more self-esteem through Deaf culture" as a way of keeping enrollment from declining further.

**DECLINING ENROLLMENT**

Enrollment has declined at these schools over the past two decades mainly due to the decline of childhood diseases

# AN INTELLECTUAL LOOK AT ASL

(i.e. Rubella) resulting in deafness. Thus, the prevailing population of postlingually deaf students was gradually replaced by prelingually deaf students. Being deafened before the age of three made the problem of educating deaf children much more complicated.

Further reduction came as a result of legislation favoring mainstreaming (PL 94-142, IDEA, Section 504 and the ADA) and state budgetary concerns (i.e. recent Nebraska school closure). However, as seen from the ASL advocates and the Culturally-Deaf leadership, the biggest threat to state residential deaf schools is the success of the Cochlear Implant (CI) technology. Audiologists and CI experts have stated on record that a residential school for the deaf is possibly the worst place for a child with a new CI *[see Menzel]*. There is no doubt that the number of deaf children with the CI is steadily increasing, perhaps even dramatically so. At this writing an estimated 10,000 to 12,000 children have the CI now. A quick look at residential school enrollment figures show that number to be in the same ball park as children with the CI. A reliable report out of Gallaudet University, estimates that 51% of deaf children will have the CI by the year 2003, but this is an underestimate -- more than half of the children now in auditory-verbal programs, not counted by Gallaudet, already have CIs, and the numbers are increasing.

**A NEW ROLE?**

So what does all this mean for residential schools for the deaf? With this question in .mind and a feeling that many associated with residential schools do not have the foggiest notion of what lies in store for them in the near future, I found it interesting that one superintendent of a residential school

# AN INTELLECTUAL LOOK AT ASL

for the deaf took the initiative to suggest a *new role for the state school for the deaf.*

In an article he wrote for *Deaf Life* (11-98) and some follow-up comments that were published in *The (Portland) Oregonian* (7-2-99), Leonard Aron, superintendent of the Washington State School for the Deaf stated: "Perhaps it is not a question of who will survive, the State School for the Deaf or *[a deaf program in]* the Public School. It may be: Can State Schools change their traditional identity and change into something new?"

Aron is suggesting that state residential schools 'adapt to a changing environment and reach out to public schools.' He says that since the majority of deaf and hard-of-hearing attend public schools where resources for deaf students are usually limited, the trained professionals at state residential schools can offer a partnership, sharing resources and expertise with all the public schools state-wide. In addition to this sharing, he suggested that 'the school become a hub for research and experiments with new teaching methods.' Aron also stated: *"I believe we don't have any future unless it is in tandem with public education."* (Emphasis in italics the author's.)

The idea of a hub for 'side-by-side' research is another interesting idea -- comparing methods head to head. But we have to weigh in another factor, the element of trust. Many feel that many residential school administrators are somewhat biased towards deaf culture and ASL and may not be bias-free enough for this idea to succeed. In addition, many strongly argue that there is no research that they can do that Gallaudet University hasn't already done. They also insist that this may be a maneuver to ensure that state funding continues to support an "ASL/Deaf Culture" cultural center and reminds us

# AN INTELLECTUAL LOOK AT ASL

that many within state deaf education programs will never voluntarily give up all that lucrative free state money.

Also curious to note is Aron's staying out of the deafness *culture vs disability* debate by focusing on what he described as the "product." However, he made it clear that 'schools for the deaf do not exist to maintain Deaf Culture' and insists that other organizations exists to fulfil that need. This is a critical point that is largely ignored by many.

## STILL, TOO MANY SERIOUS PROBLEMS TO OVERCOME

Whether one agrees with Aron or not, he has taken a brave and quite visionary position. This kind of a public stand is rather unprecedented.

Unfortunately, I have a feeling that the hard-core deaf leadership is not likely to go openly along with any plan that weakens the deaf hierarchy. On the flip side of that coin, people like myself believe that in addition to these institutions never being intended for academic learning, there are far too many other fundamental problems with residential schools to overcome. Even if it were possible, the cost to society is just too great to justify the expense, no matter how many good ideas are in the basket.

I do see one alternative that may be a bit more plausible: Integrate all the students back into their home school districts and transform the existing professional-level personnel into an efficient state agency serving deaf students statewide. These "traveling" (or itinerant) teachers of the deaf will be available to all school districts to serve as examples or in the case of a deaf teacher, role models for deaf students where in many places there are presently none. The cost savings for this suggestion is significant and will appeal to

# AN INTELLECTUAL LOOK AT ASL

many legislators who are wondering why the states are still bearing the cost of educating deaf students in the first place instead of the students' home school districts.

Indeed, the cost to society factor may very well speed up the demise of many schools. At one time when these schools were nearly the only option for educating deaf children, the high cost was perhaps justified. But today, with the numerous better and cheaper alternatives, the continued spending of taxpayer dollars on residential schools is arguably financial mismanagement.

**THE SKEPTICS ARE WARY**

While many agree a "new role" is needed, however, some researchers and professionals working with the deaf insist that these residential institutions, and even Gallaudet University for that matter, 'are not, and never were, and never will be,' regular academic facilities for the deaf. Some feel that residential schools should simply be converted to cater to groups of people (non-deaf) that really need the facilities. They also state that many school districts already have 'itinerant teachers of the deaf' who keep track of deaf students and insists that these people are professionally certified and credentialed for working in a mainstream system, qualifications that teachers from a residential school would lack. Perhaps the current intinerant programs could provide effective in-service orientation for those lacking qualification.

If residential schools continue to exist, many feel their then role should be limited to a *community* service function. Something along the lines of a deaf resource, referral, social and advocacy center, funded in part by the deaf community may be an acceptable use. Existing deaf centers can be consolidated in this facility where community activities,

# AN INTELLECTUAL LOOK AT ASL

including large events, could also be held. Unused parts of the campus can be sold or reallocated to other state agencies in return for secure and long-term funding. But many opponents of residential education insist, this "new role" should never include "academic instruction" for the deaf.

Whether or not new roles for residential schools for the deaf can succeed remains to be seen. One could argue that visionaries like Superintendent Aron actually hold the upperhand, because if the culturally-deaf leadership refuses to budge in its iron-clad traditional cultural ties to residential schools, the growth of deaf education will continue to occur outside of residential schools. And for the very reasons I outlined earlier, residential school enrollment will decline further, prompting states to continue to close them, one by one.

# AN INTELLECTUAL LOOK AT ASL

*Also available from Kodiak Media Group . . .*

| AMERICAN SIGN LANGUAGE: SHATTERING THE MYTH |
|---|
| *Edited by Tom Bertling* |

*What others are saying about this book:*

"Tom Bertling's "American Sign Language: Shattering the Myth" sounds an alarm to all parents and teachers of deaf children on the predicament in which American education of the deaf finds itself."
-Ed. Scouten, Distinguished Educator
**GALLAUDET UNIVERSITY, NTID**

"Hopefully, this collection of illuminating essays by well-known and established scholars will send a "wake-up call" to the guardians of education -- teachers and administrators -- in our schools and programs for deaf learners."
-Dr. Robert F. Panara, Professor Emeritus
**NTID/ROCHESTER INST. OF TECH.**

"Tom Bertling has done an excellent job of compiling the ignored and almost forgotten message that deaf individuals must learn to read and write English fluently, for successful careers in our modern, information-based society."
-Paulette R. Caswell, M.S.-TESL, J.D.
PhD Prgm, Int'l-Intercultural Studies
**UNIVERSITY OF SO. CALIFORNIA**

". . . indispensable, highly recommended reading for educators, administrators, parents, students and policy makers."
-James A. Cox, Editor-in-Chief
**MIDWEST BOOK REVIEW**

# AN INTELLECTUAL LOOK AT ASL

## *More about "ASL: Shattering the Myth"...*

"... In this collection of essays written by respected deaf scholars who place themselves squarely in front of the steamroller of ASL radicalism, Bertling focuses light and reason upon the internal inconsistencies, absence of scholarship, and conflict of interest of leaders of the Deaf-World.... provide(s) an important background for anyone interested in a balanced view of the current atmosphere of academic repression, especially at Gallaudet University.".
-*Thomas J. Balkany, MD, FACS, FAAP*
*Hotchkiss Distinguished Professor*
**UNIVERSITY OF MIAMI**

"Tom Bertling provides a valuable service to all educators, parents of deaf children and those interested in the continuing controversy over the use of ASL. In a unique and remarkable collection of wise and moderate voices he unmasks the politics and the mythology of ASL and yet shows respect for ASL itself. How can we thank Tom Bertling save in constant hoping that his work will be widely read and provide a moderating influence in developing educational programs..."
-*Arnold B. Adelman, Director*
**SPEECH AND HEARING FOUN-
DATION OF MASS., INC**

"... a must have, must read, must share book."
-*Nancy Tamburello, Interpreter/Reviewer*
**INDEPENDENT PUBLISHER**

"... understandable by the layperson, yet in-depth enough to be of interest to the scholar."
-*Sara Marcus, MLS, League Librarian*
**HEARING REHAB QUARTERLY**

"... thought-provoking... mandatory reading for those who wish to have a balanced understanding..."
-*Stan Foran, Editor*
**CONTACT (IRELAND)**

---

**USE ORDER FORM ON PAGE 112**

AN INTELLECTUAL LOOK AT ASL

# A CHILD SACRIFICED
## TO THE DEAF CULTURE
### *INSTRUCTIONAL-CLASSROOM EDITION*
#### By Tom Bertling

## *What others are saying about this book:*

"... A masterpiece ... gripping ... powerful ... the author's outstanding legacy to the world."
-Prof. Frances Parsons, Author
**GALLAUDET UNIVERSITY**

"... opened my eyes to a new perspective on cultural deafness...this information is vital to parents ..."
--Thomas J. Balkany, MD, FACS
Hotchkiss Distinguished Professor
**UNIVERSITY OF MIAMI**

"One hopes this book will be read by members of the deaf community with an eye towards critical self evaluation."
-Dr. Lloyd Lamb, Book Reviewer
**AMERICAN JOURNAL OF OTOLOGY**

"Tom Bertling swims where few dare to tread ..."
-Paula Bonillas, Publisher and Editor
**HEARING HEALTH**

"A remarkable new book ... at first hand, the author explains the motives of the deaf leaders ... should be required reading ..."
-Otto J. Menzel, Ph.D., Editor
**LIFE AFTER DEAFNESS**

"... a heartfelt book ... you'll be amazed ..."
-Shawn Lovley, Book Reviewer
**ALDA NEWS**

# AN INTELLECTUAL LOOK AT ASL

# NO DIGNITY FOR JOSHUA
## By Tom Bertling

## What others are saying about this book:

"Tom Bertling is the crusading knight who is challenging those fanatics, in defense of the coming generation of children who deserve a better fate than to be sacrificial pawns in a futile effort to preserve what those fanatics call "culture." If this be "genocide," make the most of it!"
-Otto J. Menzel, Ph.D., Editor
**LIFE AFTER DEAFNESS**

"Following the success of "A Child Sacrificed . . . ," Tom Bertling's second book "No Dignity for Joshua" continues the revelation by a "Deaf of Deaf" insider . . . His insights into the realities of the Deaf community, especially regarding sexual abuse of children, are disturbing. . . . Bertling's writing skills evidence the advantage of early exposure to hearing and even a short period of mainstreamed oral education. Tom Bertling is the conscience of the Deaf-World."
-Thomas J. Balkany, MD, FACS, FAAP
Hotchkiss Distinguished Professor
**UNIVERSITY OF MIAMI**

"From the oppression of deaf children to the bashing of Miss America, Bertling dissects the inner-workings of a small but powerful group who wield tremendous influence over our nation's culturally-deaf community. It is amazing to me how all this explosive material Bertling covers has missed the scrutiny of the mainstream press!"
-Paula Bonillas, Editor and Publisher
**HEARING HEALTH**

"The world needs more people like Tom Bertling to advocate on behalf of saving a crucial language for the deaf -- ENGLISH."
-Frances M. Parsons, Author
**GALLAUDET UNIVERSITY**

## USE ORDER FORM ON THE NEXT PAGE

# AN INTELLECTUAL LOOK AT ASL

## *Order these books today!*

| QUAN. | BOOK TITLE | PRICE EACH | TOTAL |
|---|---|---|---|
| | "An Intellectual Look at ASL" | $19.95 | |
| | "ASL: Shattering the Myth" | $19.95 | |
| | "No Dignity for Joshua" | $21.95 | |
| | "A Child Sacrificed" | $18.95 | |
| | Educational-Library Pack (All four books with -$3.00 discount) | $77.80 | |
| | | Handling fee | + $4.95 |
| | | TOTAL DUE | |

**MAKE CHECK OR MONEY ORDER PAYABLE TO:**
**KODIAK MEDIA GROUP**
**PO BOX 1029-J4**
**WILSONVILLE, OREGON 97070**

RUSH ORDERS MAILED WITHIN 5 BUSINESS DAYS, ADD $2.95 PER BOOK.
CANADIAN ORDERS, CHECK OR MONEY ORDER IN U.S. DOLLARS.
FOREIGN ORDERS, CHECK OR M/O IN US DOLLARS DRAWN ON A U.S. BANK.

PLEASE PRINT CLEARLY!

NAME_____

ADDRESS_____

CITY_____

STATE_____ ZIP_____ PH.(____)_____

*All orders are promptly shipped! Thank you.*